THE ME MOM

Making a Difference as an Elementary School Teacher

PETE SPRINGER

outskirts press

Table of Contents

How Did I Get Here?

How did I get here? It seems like an odd question. I'm not just learning about the birds and the bees as I approach age sixty. It is more of a question of reflection as I look back at an incredible thirty-one-year career in education. The staff I worked with are some of the best people I know in the world. The students I taught motivated me to want to be a better teacher and person. I have a lifetime of happy memories to draw on that have inspired me.

If you would have told me when I was reaching adulthood that I was destined to be a teacher for over three decades, I never would have believed it. I was a good student in high school, but I would hardly describe myself as someone who liked school. I showed up to class, did the required work, and got decent grades. When I graduated from high school, I can remember how happy I was. My jubilation, however, wasn't due to the thought of future endeavors. It was based more on the feeling that I wouldn't have to attend school anymore, and the freedom that came from not having this distraction in my life.

As the excitement of graduating ebbed, I realized that I didn't know what I was going to do with the rest of my life. When I was a kid, I dreamed about being a professional athlete. How many times did I play sports with kids in the neighborhood and fantasize about scoring the winning basket or hitting a home run in the last inning to win a game? By the time I reached adulthood, I had come to grips with my limited athletic ability, and I realized that the New York Knicks wouldn't be calling anytime soon. I began to consider other options. There was a time in high school when I began thinking about becoming a firefighter or a police officer.

My tale at that point was not that different from others my age who hadn't yet figured out their purpose in life. As graduation loomed, I remember being asked by many relatives and friends what my future plans were. The problem was I hadn't figured that out for myself. Many of my friends had already made up their minds about what direction they were going, which only added to my anxiety. I didn't turn in college applications at that point because I wasn't convinced I wanted to go to college. I had friends joining the military, others going off to college, and some going to learn a specific trade.

In my family, we were expected to all go to college. My dad had earned his doctorate and was a respected wildlife biologist who worked for the Fish and Wildlife Service. My three older brothers had all attended college. Jim, the eldest, was working as a chemist doing research work for a large pharmaceutical company. Tom was an elementary school teacher. Bill was finishing up college and was about to embark on his career as an accountant and loan officer.

I, on the other hand, had no real aspirations. It wasn't that I was lazy; I just had no idea what I wanted to do. I'm sure that this was concerning for my parents. As the summer wound down, I was working part-time at a national fast-food chain, and I decided to sign up for a few classes at our local junior college, mainly to keep my parents off my back. I took general education classes and some business classes initially. My strongest subject in school was math, and I thought about trying to find something in the field of business where I might be able to use my math skills. I didn't feel enthralled by anything I took that year, and in the last quarter, I enrolled in some police science classes. It didn't take long for me to realize that this wasn't going to be a good fit either. As the school year was nearing its end, I found a new job at a national retail store working as a stock boy and custodian. I had very few interests other than flirting with some of the cute girls who worked there and playing poker with some of my friends late into the night and early morning hours. Even though I was regularly taking their money in small stakes poker, I knew there was no future in the direction my life was going.

When I announced to my parents that I wasn't going back to college the next year, I know they were disappointed in me. At one point they sat down with me and tried to get me moving by giving me an ultimatum. I was either going to have to go out and find full-time employment, and they would start charging me rent for living at home, or I could re-enroll at college as a full-time student and thus avoid the rental expense. I didn't like either of these options, but I decided that I would go the employment route because I had no interest in continuing my studies at that point.

My dad was a good, hard-working man, and his expectations for job hunting were a little different than mine. For anyone who has tried to find a job before (this was before the invention of the Internet), you understand how disheartening the whole process can be. I came home feeling discouraged day-after-day. After weeks of searching led to nothing but futility, I recall one particularly memorable conversation with my dad about job hunting. He told me that if I wanted to find a full-time job, I should be out there "pounding the pavement" forty hours a week trying to get it. I know he only wanted the best for me, but I was already having a difficult time with all of the daily rejections.

Shortly after that, I landed a job as a tree planter. My mom had to drive me (I didn't own a car yet) to a local coffee shop at the crack of dawn where the other employees and I herded into one of two large vans and were transported to some far edge of the county. My job was simple. I wore a backpack which held five hundred young seedlings that were ready to be planted. The task was to put a hole in the ground with a foot pick they gave us, pull the seedling out of the plastic container and place it in the hole, and then tap the dirt around the sapling with my foot to ensure that it was safely anchored into the ground. Then I was to take a few more paces forward and repeat the same process until I had planted all five hundred seedlings.

The first day was uneventful, but the second day we were taken to some remote spot where we were dropped off on the side of a moun-tain. We were told to work our way down the rugged terrain until we had planted all of the seedlings. It was pouring down rain that day, but it appeared that the boss didn't think this should inhibit us in any way. I remember being out there all day long without any rain gear and just wearing a baseball cap to prevent my head from getting soaked. Even though I had a brand-new pair of work boots, it was somewhat treacherous edging down the side of this mountain because it was so steep and muddy. People were falling down left and right, unable to keep their footing. Many of my co-workers were still in sight, and several of them were finding it as hard as I to remain upright. The idea of planting trees took a backseat to survival that day. My only concern was how to navigate down the dangerous mountainside without kill-ing myself. I remember looking up at one point and observing one of my co-workers taking the saplings from his backpack and randomly throwing them in various directions. There was no way that anyone would be following behind us to verify that we were planting the young trees. Halfway down the mountainside that day, I decided that my second day would be my last. I knew that even my eco-conscious parents would not want me risking my life to plant a tree.

Shortly after this harrowing experience, I landed a new job at a daffodil bulb farm. This job required about as much brainpower as my tree planting experience. I answered an ad in the paper and showed up with a bunch of other people for a fifteen-minute train-ing session. There weren't any job interviews. If you showed up, you were hired. That ought to have given me a clue as to the skill level of this job. After our initial training session, we were quickly put to work. Each worker was assigned a long row of flowers to work on. We were told to cut the flowers at the base if they were just beginning to bloom. When you cut twenty-five flowers, you were then expected to put a rubber band around the base of the stems to hold the flow-ers together in a bunch. You set them down at the edge of your row and continued the same process. One of the other employees would come along and pick up the flowers periodically. We were paid by the total number of flowers we cut, so there was an incentive to keep moving and working all the time. As time passed, space between workers widened because some worked faster than others. I was sure I was about to make a small fortune, but as I progressed it wasn't long before my back started to hurt from all of the bending over. When I needed a break, I could rest or drink some water since we were being paid by each flower cut instead of by the time. As I checked on my co-workers, I noticed that a few people had discovered another way to reap rewards. A couple of workers were literally crossing into the rows of other people, snatching up their flowers, and putting them back in their own rows to receive credit for flowers they had not even cut.

As the days progressed, I learned to keep an eye on my row to ensure that no thievery was taking place. If it was storming outside, everyone was still expected to work. With unskilled labor like this, there were people coming and going all the time. The other major drawback, besides all of the back issues I was developing, was that my clothes were getting ruined too. Each time I cut a flower, there was a juice that began oozing from the stems. Not only was this terribly sticky, but it seemed to ruin the clothing I was wearing. If I wiped my hands off, the clothes became stained. When I got home and tried to wash everything, I discovered the stains were permanent. I just kept wearing the same two or three pairs of jeans and shirts because I didn't want to ruin everything I owned.

Many of my friends had far more masculine jobs than I at the time. I had friends who worked in mills, did construction, or cooked in a restaurant. I remember they used to tease me unmercifully about my flower picking job. That didn't bother me though. We gave each other a hard time about everything, and this was just one more thing to add to the list. I continued with this job for quite a few weeks, but the final straw for me came one day when we showed up for work and were told that we were going to be paid less for each flower we cut. Well, that didn't seem particularly fair to me, so I pulled the plug on my flower career. I did learn one valuable thing from this experience though. My boss was a very stern lady in her sixties whose management style could best be described as a militaristic one that centered on screaming at people. She wasn't that bad if you just did your job, but I learned enough to know that I wouldn't utilize this method if I ever was in a supervisory position.

My next job was at an old logging restaurant in the area. I worked the graveyard shift from 12:00 a.m. until 6:00 a.m. as a custodian. That was the first job I had in which I was mostly on my own the majority of the time. At some point in the early morning hours, bakers would come in to begin baking bread for the day.

I rarely saw anyone else except for the few instances when my boss came to check on me in the middle of the night. I'd be mopping the floor or doing some other custodial duty and look up to see a strange face peering in at me from one of the windows. I think I aged a year each time I was startled by his image! It reminded me of the uncomfortable feeling I had watching a horror film and knowing that at any instant I might receive the most unexpected shock. It was downright creepy! One of the most challenging parts of this job was trying to acclimate my body to a sleep pattern for which I was unaccustomed. I am a fussy sleeper, to begin with, and trying to go to sleep at dawn when the rest of the world was waking up was not conducive to getting a good rest.

About this time, I decided it was time to leave Humboldt County and get out on my own. One of my high school friends was living in the San Francisco Bay area, and he was looking for a roommate to help him cut his costs. I jumped at the chance to leave home, and I moved down to Daly City a few days later. I immediately took to the change in lifestyles. I loved the feeling of independence and living by my own rules. After I arrived, though, it became apparent that I was going to have to get a decent job if I was going to be able to pay my bills. Once again, finding a good job, when I possessed very few skills, was a challenge.

I began working for an organization that was selling door-to-door tickets to see the U.S. Olympic women's volleyball team play against a visiting team from China in a series of exhibition games. I had never done any door-to-door selling before, let alone in a large city like San Francisco with so many different cultures and ethnicities. We memorized a script and then were sent out to canvas particular areas of the city. It was an awful feeling to ring somebody's doorbell knowing that 95% of the time they were feeling resentful that they had to be bothered by an annoying sales pitch. I earned money when I sold tickets, so I learned how to be kind of a hustler. I once again saw the realities of doing unskilled labor. People were coming and going all the time. After a few weeks, I was one of the few regular employees still there. If you stayed for any length of time at all, you could become a manager. Managers could earn more money because they got a cut of everybody's sales, and this was my introduction to pyramid schemes. After being promoted to a manager, I had to do a lot more driving and planning. Each day I picked up and dropped off my workers. They each had a map, and I gave them specific streets to sell on. Since this was before the invention of cell phones, I had to do a lot of driving around trying to keep track of the people who were working under me.

At one point my roommate announced that he'd decided to enter the military and would be leaving soon. I knew that I'd have a hard time keeping this apartment by myself, so I began looking for other places to live. As luck would have it, my car broke down, and my bills became harder to manage. I used virtually all of my savings to get my car fixed. I continued working for the same door-to-door sales company, but things got so bad at one point that I began secretly living at our offices. Everything I owned was in my car, and it was either live out of my car or sneak back to the office where I could roll out my sleeping bag for the night. After my shift, I grabbed some dinner somewhere and then waited for everybody to leave for the evening so I could continue living in our office for another night. It was not what anyone would call a glamorous life, and I finally realized that I was going to have to move back home.

One lesson this experience taught me was to have compassion for the downtrodden. A couple of bad breaks in life and any of us can go from a life of luxury to living on the street wondering where we might get our next meal. I had the good fortune of being able to fall back on my family for security.

Having to go home after living on my own was a very humbling situation, but I've always believed that life is about learning from each experience. I could either wallow in self-pity or set a goal and start trying to achieve it. Shortly after I moved back home, things began to turn around for me. My friend's dad was a special education administrator in the county school system, and he must have heard that I was back in the area looking for a job.

My new job was being a one-on-one aide to a boy who had muscular dystrophy in a special day class. The student, who I'll refer to as "William," was at the point in his condition where he walked part of the day with the support of leg braces, and he spent the rest of his day in a wheelchair. He was a large boy, and when he fell, his teacher was not strong enough to help get him to his feet anymore. That is where I came in. If William fell, I could lift him back up, and he usually could regain his footing if he were wearing his braces. Even though he was my primary responsibility, I got a chance to work with many of the other kids in the special day class. A lot of those kids were emotionally disturbed, and there were some pretty challenging days. Part of the day, this class was integrated with the rest of the school population. They would eat lunch and have recess with the other children. I got to know lots of other kids at the school because they came over and visited me at lunch or recess. Part of each day I worked with William on a one-on-one basis. I would support him with his regular schoolwork, and then I would take him out for physical education because he was not able to do what the other kids were doing. The Humboldt County Office of Education sent over a physical therapy specialist to give me some ideas about appropriate exercises for William. Sometime during the year, I decided that I would give college another chance. I discovered that I had a talent for working with kids, and I felt good about myself when I was mentoring and counseling them.

After the summer, I returned to college, and this time felt like I belonged there for a specific purpose and goal in mind. That was the first time I seriously thought of becoming a teacher. While I took classes, I continued to work at different schools and had many other kinds of educational experiences as a teacher's aide.

Being in college now seemed to make sense because I had a reason to be there. I now had a real objective and goal in life, and I seemed to be feeling a lot happier too. After I graduated from college with a liberal studies degree, I signed up for the teaching credential program. While high school was not my favorite time in life, I found college was different. I met a lot of cool people and formed lasting friendships with others who were working toward the same goal. If that wasn't enough, I met my future wife, Debbie, in one of my education classes. In fact, things couldn't have been much better for me at that point in my life.

I have never shared most of this story with anyone, but the experiences I went through only served as further motivation. I'm sharing my story because everyone has their own life experiences. Sometimes we don't make good choices, and at other times we're just searching to make sense of it all. Children are no different. They come to school with their own life experiences, and sometimes they need teachers and other school personnel to be a stabilizing and guiding force for them. At times we need to draw upon our past struggles to offer support and wisdom to our students.

This is the story of how I fell in love with teaching and the joys and challenges that this noble profession provided to me over the course of thirty-one years. I hope that you will gain a sense that the life of a teacher is full-time and consuming, but one that ultimately can bring endless joy and satisfaction.

Introduction to Teaching

When I think about why I decided to become a teacher in the first place, I believe it primarily was because of the role models who were/are in my life. I remember visiting my Grandmother Lena in the Chicago suburbs and being fascinated by her old braille typewriter. I was too young at the time to appreciate what she was doing, but I understood that she was helping blind people by transcribing printed material to braille. My brother, Tom, had a lot of influence on me even though I probably didn't realize it at the time. Prior to 7th grade, I recall riding with my family to St. John's University in Minnesota where he was enrolling in college. I remember being upset in the car after we dropped him off because I practically idolized him growing up and knew I would miss him very much. When he became an elementary teacher upon graduating from college, I'm sure this affected me because I always admired him.

I can remember back in high school being impressed when my dad was working with some graduate students from our local university, Humboldt State. They used to refer to him as "Doc." We moved to California because my dad, who worked for the Fish and Wildlife Service, began working on a project to help restore the population of the Aleutian Cackling Goose (formerly known as the Aleutian Canada Goose). The Aleutian was a subspecies of the Canada Geese, and at one time their population was threatened. The geese still fly through our area when they are making their yearly migration from the Aleutian Islands in Alaska to the Central Valley in California.

There is no question in my mind that we all need role models, and I was incredibly fortunate to have two of the best when I began my year of student teaching at Pine Hill School. Master teachers were chosen randomly for those entering the teacher credential program in those days, and I never knew at the time that I had hit the lottery when I was assigned Cynthia Van Vleck. When I called her on the phone for the first time to set up my initial placement interview, I felt a little intimidated when she said that she was a teaching principal. In smaller schools, one of the ways a school district attempts to save money is by assigning a person to multiple positions. Our school was so tiny in those days that typically there was only one teacher per grade. Cynthia taught full-time and was allotted one-half day per week to deal with administrative duties while a substitute teacher took her place in the class. During the rest of the week, when children came to her room, she dealt with them right in her classroom. Even before I met her my initial thoughts were, "Oh boy, this is a big deal!" The endorsement and approval of a principal might determine future employment opportunities, just as a negative review might have a far-reaching impact.

After I spent the first hour in her classroom, I knew I was watching a master at work. She was in total control, and there was no doubt that the kids respected and liked her. She was firm with them, but she didn't earn their respect through direct intimidation. When she taught anything, particularly social studies, she just seemed to light up and was excited to pass on her knowledge to the kids. I enjoyed watching her teach because she was so skilled in making her classroom run smoothly. I had never heard of a teaching principal before, and it was quite impressive how she managed to deal with other children sent to her classroom in the middle of the day. The fact that she could switch roles from teacher to principal in the blink of an eye while still maintaining a regular classroom environment was amazing! She occasionally showed flashes of her incredible sense of humor with the kids.

When around her colleagues, she showed her true self. It seemed like she had an anecdote for every teaching experience and could tell a story like no other person I'd ever met. Early in my tenure as her student teacher, I decided that I wanted to become a teacher because of her. She was the perfect role model for me, and I loved everything about that experience.

In those days, student teachers were assigned a master teacher for the majority of the school year, leading up to a two-week solo teaching experience. Student teachers would also spend a month in another classroom. That was to give us experiences in more than one grade (often several years apart). In California today, I understand that they try to divide these two placements equally. While I worked in Cynthia's 6th-grade room most of the year, I had my other teaching experience with another fabulous teacher named Nancy Wheeler in her 2nd-grade classroom.

Nancy was a disciple of Dr. Madeline Hunter, a renowned educator whose research showed that effective teachers have a specific eight-step methodology when planning and presenting a lesson to maximize learning. I learned so much from Nancy in the four weeks I was with her. She skillfully involved her students in the lessons. It was a valuable experience for me to see that there was more than one way to be a good teacher. Nancy always had the kids collaborating with one another. In that respect, she was a pioneer because the predominant teaching style at the time was one in which the teacher was the most dominant force in the room. I admired everything Nancy did and enjoyed watching a real professional interacting with kids.

I was so blessed to learn from these amazing teachers during my student teaching year. Little did I know that eventually Cynthia and Nancy would become my colleagues and principals. What a fortunate experience for me to have worked with and learned from these two outstanding educators! Without their guidance, I may have never experienced the many joys that teaching provided me throughout my career.

One magical aspect of teaching is that there is no exact method or teaching style that everyone should emulate. There are specific attributes found in the best educators, but the beauty of teaching is that there are so many different ways to achieve the end goal of helping your students learn and think critically. I really appreciated Cynthia's advice to develop my style as a teacher because it took faith and trust in me to say this. Instead of saying, "Do everything my way, and you can become a successful teacher," she was giving me her permission to find my way. I took this advice to heart and believed that part of the reason most kids liked being in my room was because I wasn't a traditional teacher. For example, I enjoyed P.E. and if my class was playing a game, I usually was right there in the middle of the action. Of course, the kids found it hilarious that their middle-aged teacher was running around playing tag games with them. One advantage to playing with kids is that you can teach them about sportsmanship. I showed them to play the games hard and to the best of their ability, but I constantly reminded them that their friendships were more important than who won or lost a game.

Being a good teacher and being a good parent is not that different. Two requirements of each job are to provide children with love and discipline. Just about all children have a natural desire to please the important people in their lives. That starts with their family. One of the most important connections that you can make at the start of the school year is to let the parents/guardians know that your primary goal is to promote the welfare of their children. When parents understand that you care about the children, they are much more likely to give you support when you need their help.

When I first started teaching, I was so overwhelmed with just trying to keep my head above water regarding the kids' learning, that I don't think I sought out the help of the parents as much as I should have. My brother, a teacher of forty years in Minnesota, has a great analogy about education being like a three-legged stool. The sturdiest chairs are made up of three strong legs. The legs represent the teacher, the administration, and the home. If one of the legs is not the right length or is weaker, the chair won't be as sturdy. You may be able to sit in the chair and use it, but the chair will not be as strong without a sturdy foundation. Are you going to change every parent's attitude and involvement in their own child's education? Probably not, but does that mean that you shouldn't even try? For me, this was one of those battles worth fighting.

Becoming a good teacher is not something that happens overnight, and a beginning teacher has to realize that. With each passing month and year, teachers learn what elements are imperative to retain and what can be added to enhance their teaching. Watching a skilled teacher is a beautiful form of art. An outstanding teacher makes his/her classroom come alive. I admire artistic people, perhaps, in part, because I lack this ability. A talented teacher to me is not that different from a painter who makes a blank canvas come alive or a potter who skillfully takes a glob of clay and turns it into something useful, dependable, and even beautiful. To this day, there is nothing quite as inspiring to me as watching an educator engaging students in learning.

The art of teaching includes knowing how to get kids to pay attention and participate. I found that storytelling was one of the most successful methods to get my students to pay attention. I once had a history teacher in college who used this technique to capture the full attention of his students. He had a way of putting us into the roles of the people we were learning about, catching and holding our concentration. I looked forward to attending his class because he had a way of making history exciting and alive.

Just about everyone I know likes a good story, especially kids. Most of the stories I shared came from my own experiences as a child, parent, or teacher. Seldom were the stories fiction (I may have embellished occasionally) because I thought kids would relate better if the stories were personal. Many stories written by children's authors are written with the intention to teach a lesson. The same was true with my stories. They often prompted students to share their own experiences because my story reminded them about something similar in their lives. It is essential to give students a chance to respond, but more often than not, when their excitement was evident, I would have them turn to their journals to capture their thoughts. That was a great way to transition into the next subject after giving them a set amount of time to write. Some students would be frustrated if they had more they wanted to write about when the time ended. Those who needed more time could take their journals home that night to finish up. The day after writing in the journals, I encouraged them to share if they wanted to. Every class typically had children who seldom or never wanted to share their writing, while there were others who always wanted the spotlight. By creating a non-threatening environment where kids could share their thoughts and feelings without fear of ridicule, even the shy children began to open up as the year progressed. Growing up, I was a shy kid at times, so I could relate to how these children were feeling.

Part of the reason that people are shy is biological, but sometimes individuals become withdrawn because of their own life experiences. When someone is ridiculed or made fun of in a mean or cruel manner, I believe it affects the way that person acts in the future. We moved several times when I was growing up, and I started high school after moving to California. I withdrew more because many of my classmates had established their friendships, and it was easier for me to fade into the background. If I could repeat this part of my life, I would put myself out there and become involved more in drama and sports. Finding your niche often has to do with finding other people who share the same passion for the things that you like. I have seen this dynamic with musicians, artists, and athletes over the years. It wasn't until I started college that I blossomed and became much more confident and outgoing. I liked myself better once I became a more fearless guy who was willing to take more chances. I shared this story with some of my shyer students and felt especially satisfied when I was able to bring this quality out of some of my kids. Sometimes near the end of a school year, I had the students write about their memories of the year. I felt proud when one of them wrote something like, "This year I learned not to be so afraid to speak in front of my class."

There are always a few kids who don't want to share because they aren't ready to take that risk yet. In situations like this, I looked for ways to get there by taking baby steps. If I could get such children to accept having their work read aloud in class, then that was the first hurdle to clear. I might do this by catching children a few minutes before class and compliment them on their writing. At this time, I might even mention privately, "I hope you decide to read your journal today. It is excellent." Other intermediate steps might include asking children if they would stand up with a friend or have another student read their journal. I might even ask students' permission to read their journals aloud if they didn't want to share. That generally worked because they seemed to feel less vulnerable when someone else was reading their thoughts and words.

As the year went on, many students felt safer and were willing to take a more significant risk. Having children share their thoughts with a trusted friend or in a one-on-one situation was another inter-mediate step. Even with all of these modifications, you may have a few kids who still don't want to participate. While I understood this, I also was unwilling to accept it. I might start class one day by telling the kids that one of the students wrote something so awesome, that I had decided to read it to them. At some point, you may have to give students a deadline to share their writing aloud. Try telling a student to find something to share in the next week. This provides a child with an expectation but also gives each student a chance to get used to this scary idea.

One thing that I always told my student teachers was that teach-ers are the biggest thieves in the world. I'm not trying to say that educators don't have a sense of morality. I merely mean that most teachers are wise enough not to try and reinvent the wheel when they see something that they think will work for them. Some of my principals liked to have staff meetings in our classrooms. One thing I would sometimes do in one of these meetings, notably if the gather-ing weren't very stimulating (staff meetings can be boring at times), was to observe things in that teacher's classroom. Something would often catch my attention, and I'd ask my colleague about it after the meeting.

While teaching has changed dramatically in some ways over time, in other regards, it is very much the same. Students have always wanted to feel safe and cared for at school. I believe that one of the most significant predictors of children's success, or lack thereof in school, has to do with their relationship with the teacher. I wanted the kids to know that they were like my second family. When one of them did well on something (any learning experience), I felt proud. When one of them made a poor decision, I felt disappointed. Regardless of any mistakes that they made, I wanted my students to know that I would continue to love and care for them. Rather than being angry when a child took someone else's property or lied about something at school, I looked at these situations as opportunities to teach. I believed that it was essential to tell the kids when I made similar mistakes growing up. That didn't mean telling kids about every youthful indiscretion or mistake that I ever made, but it does show kids that, even as adults, we should always try to better ourselves. Just because we are teachers doesn't mean we have everything figured out and that we're perfect today. We all make mistakes from time to time. The smart people are the ones who learn from their mistakes.

Classroom management is one of the most critical skills that effective teachers need to have if they are going to be successful. Knowing how to diffuse a situation without the use of intimidation is so essential. When a student acted up, I tried to talk with that student privately. This often occurred after I gave the student a time-out. If you get into power struggles with individual students, especially in front of their classmates, you are setting them up for failure. Many kids will be more prone to talk back and act in a nonconforming manner if you challenge them in front of their peers. That is especially true as kids become older and begin to question authority more.

What teachers do and how they act is being watched and learned by children at all times. If we lose our calm, we are teaching them that it is okay to behave in this manner when something is not going right. We are regularly tested as teachers to set a good example for our students. If a child was rude or disruptive, I firmly let that student know that I wasn't going to tolerate that behavior, but I tried very hard to do this in a way that didn't humiliate the student.

Setting up Your Classroom

When the school year gets underway, it is challenging to make significant changes to the classroom. You will pour most of your energy into the curriculum, and this leaves little time for focusing attention on the learning environment. That is why it is crucial to invest some time before the school year begins.

Throughout your career, you will likely experiment with different classroom arrangements. Taking photos of the classroom is helpful when trying to recall different layouts. Gathering ideas from other teachers also aids in this process.

There are many things to be considered when arranging the children's desks and other work areas. When I began teaching, most teachers commonly placed their students in rows. Best educational practices now call for students to collaborate and help one another, so it makes sense to organize the class in pairs or small groups. Our reading program emphasized partner reading and group work, so placing the kids in sets of four facilitated this nicely. The type of furniture that your school owns obviously will influence some of your decisions.

When developing the seating chart, a great resource will be a visit with the previous year's teacher(s). That allows you to find out other information about your incoming students besides what is already available in their cumulative educational files. Even though we often had three classes per grade, once I got my class list, I made it a point to visit each teacher. You find out about each student's strengths and weaknesses academically, but you also will get information about students' personalities and behaviors. Some children can work with just about anybody, but there are also those who will be more successful if you put them with the right partner or group. Some guesswork is involved, but it is invaluable when a former teacher says, "Whatever you do, don't put 'Teddy' with 'George.' They talk all the time and get silly together." While students mature and grow over time, I often found a lot of truth in the information that I gathered.

If children are new to the school, call their previous teacher from the former school to learn whatever you can about them ahead of time. You may also inherit some kids who have been in a home-schooled situation. Try to get whatever information you can, but keep in mind that some parents don't have a good handle on where their child is academically. There have been times when I received home-schooled children, and the parent indicated, "Jill is so good at math! I'm just amazed at what a great math student she is!"

Sometimes the reality was that "Jill" was one of my lower achieving math students. The parent wasn't trying to be deceptive, but rather lacked any basis for comparison. You may also find that the child's behavior is completely different with you than with the parent. Of course, we can say that of all children. These differences can be either positive or negative. There were occasions at conference time when I told parents how impressed I was with how hard their child worked in class. At times the parents saw the same thing at home, but sometimes they would snicker and say something like, "Well, I'm glad he works hard at school because we can't get him to do anything at home! Maybe you could talk to him because he'll listen to you."

There were also times where I'd tell the parents that their child had a hard time working with others, and they grew defensive. It takes skill and experience to diffuse situations such as that. I would bring up my challenges as a fellow parent as a means of letting them know that we all struggle from time to time when it comes to raising kids.

A final point I would like to make is that when a child interacts with you, it can be different compared to the previous year's teacher. It is important to start your teacher-student relationship without any preconceived notions regarding the child's attitude based only on an earlier teacher's comments. Although this can help you develop a strategy; at the same time, you wouldn't want to be judged solely on a negative comment made by one parent. Consulting previous teachers can help to eliminate some potential problems by gaining insight. For example, you may learn to seat a child near the front of the room due to vision problems. Knowing this ahead of time allows you to help the child be successful. Perhaps some changes in family dynamics occurred in the previous year, such as a parent remarrying, divorcing, or returning home after spending time in prison. That is the type of information that can better prepare us to support the child by being observant for any signs of difficulty or struggles.

Determining the placement of your work area is almost as important as the students. Be close enough to the kids so that you can work with small groups of children while also keeping an eye on the rest of the class. If possible, I preferred to situate myself in a position to make eye contact at all times.

Try different arrangements because you may end up trying something that works much better than what you were doing previously. Perhaps you try something new that doesn't work as well as you hoped. Then either go back to what you were doing or experiment with something altogether different. Make these changes after school or on a weekend when you have the time to determine if your idea is physically possible. I once taught in a portable classroom connected to a similar movable structure. The room was long and narrow, limiting arrangements I could configure. Two trailers together also made for a very noisy environment. If my students were working quietly and the neighboring teacher's class began moving around a lot, it was very distracting for my students, and I'm sure it was the same for my colleague.

I have also had a portable building serving as my classroom without any running water. What a pain that was! Kids get thirsty all the time, so we had a large bottled water container. Dealing with frequent spills of water that missed the target of paper cups or individual water bottles was a constant challenge. Can you imagine trying to teach an art project involving painting without running water? What about cleaning everything up when the project is finished? Working in a portable classroom meant that the bathrooms were not close. You can't have children coming and going or disappearing ten minutes at a time. It was less than an ideal situation, but you learn to be flexible in education!

My last classroom was nearly ideal with lots of storage and space. Being centrally located was a huge plus, and the office, library, playground, cafeteria, and bathrooms were nearby. However, the downside was that the room was stuffy. Our classroom seemed to have classes passing by all day long as students went to lunch and recess at different times. Picture Grand Central Station here! Throughout the day the windows were opened and closed, as we tried to balance a stuffy room versus outside noise and bees regularly flying in. Although I brought this to the principal's attention, the bottom line was that we had to learn to deal with it.

Another area to consider when planning your classroom layout is to provide a space where you can work with a small group of students away from the rest of the class. I had a semicircular table which fit nicely in the area, and I could position my chair in a manner that allowed me to work with a few children while keeping an eye on the remainder of the class.

Setting up centers or stations requires planning time. I kept an ongoing jigsaw puzzle in one area of the room at a table where four to five kids could go if they finished their work early. I had places where the kids could go to read independently, located near their book bags. (Kids had designated books placed in plastic bags that were easily accessible.) The point of book bags was to eliminate kids gathering around the bookshelves "looking for a book" for ten minutes. I allowed them to come in early before school to trade the books from their book bag.

In my last two years of teaching, the second and third grades shared a rolling cart with a class set of computers. When the cart was in my room, there needed to be a space where it could fit, and the computers could be charging when they weren't in use. One of the things that my grade level colleagues and I were still trying to work out during those years was to develop a schedule so that we shared the computers equally. One of the problems that we frequently ran into was the need to have three or four laptop computers at certain times in the day. We all were using Accelerated Reader as a supplemental reading program, and the kids who finished their work early would often want access to a computer where they could take a brief assessment on a book they were reading. The challenge we faced was making this happen while also providing the rolling cart of the full set of class computers to a teacher who needed all of them for a class assignment.

Mobility is essential in the arrangement of the classroom, ensuring that there are no bottlenecks near doorways. Even with kids working in groups or pods, it is still important to allow them enough space to move around comfortably while making allowances for adequate personal space.

A separate area for students' coats and backpacks with individual compartments is vital in keeping the classroom safe. I inherited a wooden structure from another teacher bolted to the wall and out of the way that was perfect for storage. Allowing kids to keep their backpacks and coats on the back of their seats creates a tripping hazard, as they inevitably end up on the floor. The custodian installed a coat rack, and the problem was solved.

Making personal purchases of some necessities benefits you in the long run. Buying an excellent electric pencil sharpener each year eliminated crowds of children hovering around the manual pencil sharpener, while kids futilely tried to sharpen broken pencils. One of my classroom jobs was to have a student sharpen new pencils. When a pencil broke, a child could put it in the "to-be-sharpened" container and grab a sharpened pencil from the "sharp-pencil-box" without wasting any time.

After recesses, many kids wanted to go to the office to get an ice pack for some ailment. I used to joke that I could open a side business at school renting ice packs. The ice pack was the miracle cure for most physical problems. Kids asked for them for whatever was bothering them. Rather than fighting this time-waster each day at school, I decided to get a set of ice packs to put in my mini-refrigerator in class. Keeping students in class ensures that more learning takes place. The mini-refrigerator also housed my snacks as well.

Another time saver and strategy to keep kids in the classroom was to invest in a small portable copy machine that I placed in my room. During a typical school year, you will make thousands of copies. At my school, there was a copy limit set on the two public copiers we had in the teacher's break room. When one of the copiers broke down, multiple people could be waiting to use the lone working copier. There were so many times when I just needed to make an extra copy or two of something. I could do it without losing valuable class time sending kids out to have a copy made.

Place things like class or school rules, classroom jobs, and educative bulletin boards in areas that are visible from the students' desks. At the beginning of the year, I posted the routine of what I wanted my students to do if they finished their assignments. Having a list of choices posted will cut down on students asking what they are supposed to do when they finish their work. That translates into fewer interruptions for you when working with a small group of kids.

Teachers will often make arrangements with one another about sending students who may need time-outs to another teacher's classroom. That usually occurs when students need to complete an assignment. Perhaps the student procrastinated instead of finishing the task. This type of working relationship with a small group of fellow teachers may result in students showing up unexpectedly. Since you may be in the middle of your own lesson when a student arrives, it is crucial to have a designated spot ready for these "guests" to minimize interruptions. The ideal location is far away from the rest of the class.

Just direct the student where to sit and continue your lesson.

Whatever your routines, they need to be in place before the first day of school. The only thing I wanted on desktops was a pencil box for pencils and other small supplies. When the back-to-school sales started each year, I picked up small, plastic pencil boxes. If I bought them at the right time, I spent a dollar or less. Perhaps you feel like this should not be your financial burden. On the other hand, I always had some kids whose families were so needy that they never came in with new school supplies of their own. Wanting to teach the kids my routines from day one, the children started their day with a pencil box on their desk and ended school by picking up after themselves. Depending on the type of desks that the students have, direct them where their supplies should go. By insisting that small items belong in pencil boxes, we eliminated those very things ending up on the floor.

Other routines beginning on the first day of class included what to do each morning when they walked into the classroom: Place homework in the designated spot, put coat/backpack in their cubby, make sure sharp pencils are ready, and have an expectation that they will begin working on their morning warm-up. The morning warm-up usually consisted of a small set of problems for them to work on in math or language arts while I was taking roll and other necessary things in preparation for the day. Having a small academic assignment waiting for the kids when they entered the classroom each day helped to create a good working environment.

Working with Students

Whenever I think back to what made my career truly special, the first thing that comes to mind are students I was touched by in some fashion. Running a classroom is like being boss of your own company. In fact, in some ways, I ran my class like a business. When I taught 5th and 6th grades, I gave the kids paychecks once a month based on their productivity. I tried to develop a system that was based more on recognizing their effort and taking responsibility rather than only rewarding the kids who were inherently smarter. Not every child in the class received the same amount in their paycheck because not all of the students were equally productive. I tried to connect real life with my classroom whenever possible. Those kids who were faithful about doing their homework and coming to class ready to work earned more than the students who were lazy or irresponsible. My message to my students was that they were ultimately responsible for their life achievements. Many kids have much greater advantages solely because of their parents' socioeconomic status, but living in a wealthy family is no guarantee that a person will be successful or happy. Being raised in a loving family and being taught the importance of core values, such as a strong work ethic and taking responsibility for your actions, is a more significant motivator and a better predictor of future success.

The kids in my class could save their play money or use it to purchase things from our class auctions. I worked with a local bank and was provided with bank books so that students could keep track of their own money. Every three months or so, I would hold an auction in my class whereby the students could either buy items by being the top bidder or choose to save their funds. When I was about to hold an auction, I just went to a dollar store and did some creative shopping. After working with children for so many years, I had a pretty good sense of the things kids liked. The items I bought, or which were donated, provided my students with a fun activity that held their interest.

The auctions were a great learning experience. Some kids were quite apprehensive to bid at first, but things generally got going fast and furious after the students saw how the process worked. One of my rules was that they had to raise the bid at least $.05, so immediately this brought mental math into the activity. There were almost always a couple of kids who got caught up in the moment and regretted buying something they didn't want. I taught my students in advance how to write checks and how to maintain a check register. If a student had the winning bid on an item, I would have the child write me a check for it. The kids would not get to claim their prize until they had correctly executed the check and figured out their new balance. I also kept records of their totals to ensure they were doing their math correctly. Some kids (this is normal behavior for kids of this age) would start bidding partly because they wanted to jack up the price for one of their classmates. Of course, sometimes this backfired, and the student who kept upping the bid would end up purchasing an item he/she didn't want. I had students who lacked the self-discipline to try to get the best deal and merely bid their whole bankroll. Often, when children regretted their decisions, they would try to sell their item back to me. I stayed firm and wouldn't allow the return of purchased things. Sometimes kids bid their entire amount of money and were outbid by another child who had more. All of these were valuable life lessons.

Observing human nature in different children is a fascinating aspect of teaching. My wife was a preschool teacher and later a preschool director. We enjoyed looking over my new class list each year because I almost always inherited a few of her former students. She

would tell me about the students she remembered. They were between three to five years of age when she first encountered them, yet
nearly all of her observations were similar to what I witnessed several
years later, both positive and negative. It probably isn't so surprising
that the similarities persisted; however, it was disheartening to think
that a child born into poverty or enduring a childhood without positive role models, was much more likely to perpetuate the cycle, as
was a child raised in a loving home with strong support. Of course,
the children don't get to choose what their living environment will be.

While some children are born into more stable situations than
others, many remarkable kids overcome the obstacles of dysfunction
in their lives and go on to do great things. They can change their community in positive ways despite having a difficult childhood.

As a long-time teacher in the same school, I developed relationships with many of my students' families. New students would regularly tell me that I taught one of their relatives. Every year, toward the
end of my career, I ended up teaching the children of former students.
To hold a parent-teacher conference with an adult who used to be
one of my students was a strange experience. Not surprisingly, many
of these kids inherited personality traits and habits that I recognized
from when their parents were my students. My long-time colleagues
and I joked about what we'd like to say to these former students,
"Your child has a hard time remaining focused during the lessons,"
or, "He has some difficulty working with other children in a group. In
fact, he reminds me of you!"

A lot of kids coming into my class said they had hoped I would
be their teacher. I'd like to say that this was because I was such a great
teacher, but the real reason was that many of them had seen me doing
something silly at an assembly and had decided that this must be the
way I acted all the time. I enjoyed having fun with my students, but
I also took my job very seriously. Each day was a new opportunity to
try and make a positive impression. At the end of the year, I wanted
my students to feel special, loved, and cared for by me. I wanted them
to know that they would be my students for life and that if they ever

needed something, I would be there for them.

The obvious question is, how does one go about connecting with students? Well, it starts on the first day of school. Try to get to know the students and understand the things that are important to them. Before the end of the first day of school, I would share a letter that I had written to my students about myself. I told my class about the things that were meaningful in my life. The letters varied over the years depending on what had happened that last summer or what I was interested in at the time. Pretty much every year, though, I told my students about my family and the things that I liked to do in my free time. I then gave them a homework assignment (Yes, I did give my students homework on the first day of school.) asking them to write back and tell me whatever they wanted about themselves. What they chose to say to me was fascinating. Some kids opened up immediately, and others were a little more guarded. Many children wrote about their families, their pets, hobbies, or something fun they had done that past summer. I always gave the kids the opportunity to share their letters with the class if they wanted to the following day. This simple act helped me learn a lot about the kids right away. Most children immediately fit into one of three groups:

1. Children who loved being the center of attention and were thrilled to have the opportunity to share in front of the class.
2. Children who wrestled with wanting to share but were kind of scared to do it.
3. Children who had no desire to share or even have me read their letters aloud to the class.

I was a shy kid, who later became a big ham, so I certainly could relate to all of these groups. There was a time when I would do just about anything besides speaking publicly. I was very familiar with feeling self-conscious in front of a large group of people, and one of my goals was to help my students develop more self-confidence. I told stories about my own life because I knew many of the kids would be able to relate to those feelings.

One of the stories I told my students was about overcoming fears. I told them about my fear of the high dive or of going on a scary amusement park ride, and the pride I felt when I conquered one of my phobias. The kids could relate to that and then wanted to share their own experiences. This was the time when I had the kids bring out their journals. I wanted them to write when they were excited, rather than when they felt it was a task. The one question I wanted to avoid at all costs was, "How much do we have to write?" If they asked that question, then they were approaching it as an unpleasant job rather than something eagerly anticipated. The question I tried to elicit from my students was, "Can we write about this in our journals?" I wanted my students to learn that writing was a sacred time.

During this period, I was also writing. I wanted to convey that I looked forward to writing, and the only distractions I would allow was questions about spelling or structure. If they finished and asked me to read their work, I told them that I needed to complete my writing and that I was looking forward to reading their thoughts after school. Once they finished, they were trained to find something quiet to do so as not to be a distraction for the children still writing. That might mean reading a book quietly, working on a prior assignment, working on extra credit, or drawing something related to their journal writing. There weren't many times that I expected complete silence in the room, but journal writing was one of them.

Spend time teaching your students the routines of your classroom. If you want things done a certain way, then practice these routines within the class. Don't just tell them what you expect to see; rehearse, role play, and act out these situations until it becomes second nature. In the long run, spending a little extra time, in the beginning, will make all the difference throughout the year. That is also the time to set boundaries for acceptable behaviors. Every year I witnessed a bit of apprehensiveness from students on the first day, but by the second day, as children felt safer and more comfortable in my classroom, some would begin to act out.

Regaining control after allowing inappropriate behavior is very difficult, so nip it in the bud. It is your responsibility to reaffirm what acceptable behavior is. It is much easier to be firm, fair, and consistent at all times. Children like surprises regarding some things in life, but they feel reassured and safe when the classroom environment remains steady.

Personal responsibility is a core expectation. Students should perform jobs to keep the classroom running smoothly. They can be assigned to sharpen pencils, pass out materials, and help with many other tasks that contribute to the classroom while providing a lesson in responsibility. Most elementary students are thrilled to help out in their class.

Over 50% of the kids in our school also attended the after-school program, which was a place where they could get homework help, exercise, take part in enrichment activities, and even get something nutritious to eat. Sometimes I would get one or more of my students out of the after-school program for tutoring or to take part in a classroom job. Many viewed this as a special privilege rather than a chore. If kids asked me if they could come back after school to help out, a precondition always involved the completion of their homework.

Setting both individual and class goals are important because some kids buy in right away while others take longer to get on board. During the second half of my career, the entire class had to work together to accomplish a goal. I refer to this as "positive peer pressure." Each day they completed their homework, I added a letter toward spelling a word(s) written on a high visibility area on the whiteboard. They grew excited because each letter added on was one step closer to achieving their goal. They learned that it took a team working together to earn popcorn or whatever perk they were trying to reach. I thanked those who were making positive changes when I witnessed improvements in their work habits or behavior. Their peers would also recognize these changes by clapping for those students who were improving.

Occasionally, there would be days when only one or two students wouldn't have their homework done, and there would be a collective disappointment from the remainder of the class. While I didn't permit others in the classroom to harass those students, I often could tell that the children who didn't finish their homework felt a sense of obligation to do better.

I took great pride in helping students develop better habits, especially those who began the year without assuming much responsibility for their homework. When I had students like this, I first tried to understand why the work wasn't getting done rather than becoming frustrated with them. Once the reasons were understood, the solutions weren't too hard to figure out. Some kids just never had a parent who put a priority on this before. Other students had many extracurricular activities in which they were involved. Some children struggled because they lived in more than one house during the week with different sets of expectations for the separate households. One set of parents would make schoolwork a top priority, and the child's other set of parents might never worry about it. I had a few kids who lived in situations where the parents already had an ax to grind with schools because of negative experiences they might have had when they were in school. Many schools have after-school programs, and ideally, the work should get done there, if the adult in charge has excellent classroom management skills.

The best form of positive reinforcement given by teachers is praise. Elementary students have a strong desire to please the adults in their lives (parents, grandparents, guardians, teachers, etc.). When I told a student that I intended to call his parent that night because I was so proud of him, a huge smile formed on the student's face nearly every time. The majority of my contacts with parents were positive. Communication came in the form of phone calls, a personal note, positive e-mail, or speaking to them in person before or after school on the school grounds. Sometimes I contacted parents privately, but at other times I would ask the student to stay in the room for a minute at recess and call the parent so that my student could hear the praise. The parents were thrilled. At times I even put the child on the phone to listen to the immediate feedback from home. I kept a record of these contacts with parents. Does this take some extra time? Absolutely! Was it worth the trouble of recording these contacts? An emphatic YES! Every student should be recognized during the year for positive behaviors and work habits. One of the most overlooked groups of kids are those who consistently do their job day after day. We must recognize them. It is easy to focus all of your energy on those kids who have issues with homework, self-discipline, or behavior, but the students who are responsible, turn in high quality work, or behave appropriately need reinforcement too. I used to tell my class about former students I hired to work for me. They babysat our son when he was little, took care of our pets when we were on a trip, and did yardwork for me. Although I didn't reveal any names, I did tell them about the kind of people I wanted working for me. I reinforced why being responsible and self-disciplined are essential, and I used this as one example of how people recognize these types of qualities in others.

I do think that it is possible for parents or schools to provide too many rewards for kids. In my family, everyone was expected to contribute to the running of the household. As a youngster, this meant I had certain chores that I was supposed to do every week. These were things (clean my room, clean up after myself, wash the dishes) that I was expected to do without anticipating any reward. If I wanted to try to earn some money, then I went to my parents and asked them what I could do beyond my regular duties. They often found something for me to do for very nominal pay. It is interesting when you grow to adulthood and are one day faced with many of those same decisions your parents had concerning the raising of children.

Whenever a teacher or parent disciplines a child, the most critical part is not the revoked privilege, but the discussion that should take place. The message must be clear. If a child is punished merely out of anger or frustration without any dialogue or learning taking place, the act is pretty much pointless. When we disciplined our son (fortunately, we did not have to do this too often), we always ended up our discussions by talking about what happened, hugging him, and reminding him that we loved him. When at school, I spoke to the students and let them know I was glad they were in my class. One expectation in our meeting was that students articulated why they received consequences and how they would avoid situations like this in the future. If one of the kids lost his temper in the middle of a recess game, I would ask him why he thought I took basketball away for two days. I tried to get him to tell me a strategy he could use if a situation like this arose again.

Each day I tried to greet my students at the door, say goodbye to them at the end of the day, and remind them of any tasks that they had for homework. I walked out with the children being picked up to find opportunities to interact with their parents.

I like to joke and am a bit of a teaser. While I often joked around with my students, I always tried to be conscious of what and how I said something. Human beings are sensitive, and words do have the power to hurt or heal. Using sarcasm, especially with younger children, is not the way to tease a child. When hearing inappropriate teasing from others, I used this as an opportunity to show them the difference between what is playful and what is hurtful.

For example, during the year I usually had some incident in which someone made fun of the way a student looked. If I questioned a student about why she did this and the response was, "Gosh, I was just kidding," I would try to help that child understand that this type of teasing is inappropriate and hurtful. Teasing in elementary school, in particular, should not belittle a person. I sometimes gave a list of made up scenarios to see if the class felt each of these situations was "friendly teasing" or "mean teasing." The teasing I prohibited were making fun of someone's person (either the way they looked or dressed) or teasing another child about having a crush on someone. These were common areas of teasing that provoked negative responses.

One special tradition that I started in my classroom was to recognize a "star student" each week. Although this was one of the class jobs, it was more like a position of honor. I sent a note home with the child the week before, explaining to the parents what would be happening. The kids had the option of bringing in pictures of themselves and telling the class a little bit about the photos. Sometimes children didn't have many photos to share, or in a couple of rare cases, I had children who were recently adopted and had no pictures or memorabilia from childhood. I didn't force anyone to participate, but most enjoyed the recognition. For some of the timid children, this was a great way to get them to join in a public speaking situation. Most kids enjoyed being the center of attention, and I merely facilitated the process.

When children completed their presentations, their photos went up on a bulletin board for the rest of the week. The star student also received certain privileges. The child got to be first in line all week (This is important to many elementary students). On Thursday I had lunch with the star student and one of his/her friends. I had to institute a rule that when the child decided who to invite, they let me know, at which time they were no longer to change lunch buddies. That was because I had students ask more than one friend for lunch, and we ended up with some very upset children. Occasionally, students would use this privilege to manipulate their friends by telling others they would not be chosen to be a lunch buddy if they played with another child at recess. It is important to always pay attention to the classroom dynamics that are going on around you.

Early in the week I also sent a traveling bag home with the star student. The student would return with my suitcase on Friday loaded with things that he/she wanted to share with the class. The student chose these items, but I asked the parents to help guide the child. Many brought in an assortment of things, but most kids shared trophies they earned playing sports or from other feats. A lot of kids brought in items from a hobby they had. Other children liked to bring in mementos from trips they had taken. Several children would bring something with sentimental value, such as a baby blanket. I think the kids found it fun to carry my bag home and to load it with mysterious things. The star student also was the only student who got to share, and this made it more special. It was just a glorified sharing experience, but it was a very successful technique in helping my students feel more comfortable speaking in front of an audience. I also allowed the star student to choose P.E. for the class on Friday. The student would often choose one of the more popular games that we had already played, but sometimes I was introduced to new games by the star student.

I always believed that it was important to give my students many public speaking opportunities. When I was in high school, I had to take a speech class during my junior year. Since I had minimal experience in this area, I remember how scary it was. During one of my first speeches in front of the class, my knees began shaking involuntarily. I remember my high school teacher telling us at the time that public speaking was the number one fear of adults in America. That made an impression on me, and when I became an elementary teacher, I vowed to give my students many opportunities, so they wouldn't have to go through what I experienced.

One of the regular public speaking assignments I gave my class later in the school year was to do a demonstration speech. That was a good experience for nearly everyone and provided them with a safe, non-threatening public speaking opportunity. I taught the kids a simple four-step process on how to give a demonstration. First, they introduced the subject by asking the audience a question or telling a short anecdote related to the topic. Next, they stated what they were going to teach the audience. Then, they conducted the demonstration. Finally, they took questions from the audience at the conclusion of their presentation. The content wasn't nearly as relevant as the experience itself, but there were some entertaining demonstrations. Kids showed their classmates anything from how to change a bike tire to how to put up a tent. Many kids gave arts and crafts lessons, cooking demonstrations, chemistry exhibitions, and a variety of other things. One student, whose dad was a firefighter, showed us how to put out a pan fire with a fire extinguisher. One boy brought his lawn mower to school and demonstrated how he operated it in his lawn care business. Another child, whose family ran a dairy farm, actually showed the kids how to milk a cow. Another student demonstrated how to gut and clean a fish. The demonstrations were often fascinating, but the most important thing is they gave each of the kids a chance to be the "expert." Many students involved the rest of the class. One student presented a step by step demonstration of how to draw a monster truck. Another student showed how to use chopsticks. After he had finished his demo, he gave each of his classmates a pair of chopsticks to practice with by serving them some cooked rice.

One of the extra things I tried to put into my schedule was an attempt to attend an extracurricular activity of each of my students at some point during the year. Taking on something this ambitious wasn't possible for me some years. Part of what determined if I was able to do it had to do with the age of my son. After he started driving and then went off to college, I could devote more time to this kind of thing. A logical question might be, "With all the things that a teacher has to do already, why would you create more things to do for yourself?" My answer is that I found it to be one of the easiest ways to benefit my teacher/parent relationships.

Parents genuinely appreciated the extra effort I made in supporting their children, and the paybacks I got were enormous. The goodwill you create from this simple gesture makes it worthwhile. I found that the parents were almost always supportive of me if they trusted me, and this little bit of extra effort paid off. I would tell the parents at Back to School Night and in the weekly parent note that I would be happy to come to one of their child's activities if invited. Many parents would then make a copy of their child's schedule, and I was often able to work it so that I could attend an activity in which several of my students were involved at the same time. It was fun to see my students in a different environment, and I knew it meant a lot to them. When children feel like their teacher cares about them, they will try harder in return. One of the most enjoyable aspects of my retirement has been that some of my former students still send me copies of their sports' schedules, music concerts, and other various extracurricular activities. I find it touching that they care enough about me to stay in contact, and of course, I still try to make every attempt to attend one of their events.

Some of the most important lessons that kids learn in school aren't those things that come from a textbook or are part of the regular curriculum. Over the course of a typical school year, a child should learn how to deal with other people when they have a conflict or disagreement. You need to provide kids with a chance to express their concerns in a manner that doesn't disrupt the flow of a regular school day. It is not the job of a teacher to be the judge and jury for every problem that arises. What you do need to provide is a method by which students can solve their problems because conflict resolution is a necessity in any organized society. The majority of the issues that my students had occurred on the playground, which is the least controlled environment at school. With only a couple of supervisors trying to oversee the many activities and interactions occurring between children every recess, it is best if children can work out conflicts and differences among themselves rather than adults trying to act as problem solvers for them. A real sign of maturity is when children can come up with solutions on their own to the problems they face. There is curriculum designed to help address this. Much of it gets kids role playing and trying to come up with win/win solutions in which both sides compromise a little to help solve a problem.

Not all children have the maturity or ability to solve problems on their own, so providing children with an avenue for addressing their issues or concerns is invaluable. To help understand the problem without taking away from classroom time, have the children fill out a problem sheet (See Appendix). That gives them a chance to express the problem without making everything come to a grinding halt in class. A problem sheet can be simple and straightforward with a place for their name, the date that the problem occurred, and the solution used to try to solve the problem. That places the responsibility back on the child instead of making the teacher the "great problem solver."

I kept problem sheets over the course of the year as it was an excellent way to collect data about the kids who found themselves repeatedly having conflicts with other children. Some students fill out problem sheets all the time, while others may rarely or never fill one out. As I told my students, I was much more likely to pay attention to a concern of a child who seldom wrote problem sheets rather than the one who turned them in daily. What was interesting was that besides the children who had many social interaction problems, there were children who did things under the radar that I picked up on as a result of having this resource.

When a child completed the problem sheet and turned it into me, I wanted my class to understand that I wouldn't necessarily look at their problem sheet at that instant, but I would try to look at the issue before the next recess. Sometimes what the kids thought were "problems" were so insignificant that they weren't worth addressing. I also had kids who didn't want to be bothered with filling out a problem sheet, but then I assumed that the problem couldn't be all that important if they didn't want to take the time to write about it.

Many times, after reading the problem sheet, I realized that I needed to get a couple of kids together to talk out a situation. I tried to sit down with the kids privately at a recess or lunch break and get them to listen to each other. Another benefit of waiting a little while to do this was that the kids were often calmer and able to discuss a situation with a higher degree of maturity than if I had tried to deal with it immediately. I often noted that both kids could have handled the situation better after listening to their versions. There were situations when one child was clearly in the wrong, and I might need to impose some consequence. However, I always looked at situations like these as opportunities to teach rather than merely times to punish kids. The most important thing was having the kids learn from the incident so that they would know what to do if faced with a similar situation in the future. It was vital for them to see and hear something from another child's point of view and understand that two people could view the same situation quite differently. At the very least, I wanted them to take the other student's feelings into consideration.

Another method for problem-solving was to hold a class meeting periodically. I was not always great about following through with these or finding the time to hold them, but I learned they were one of the most effective ways to deal with more substantial classroom problems. When multiple children were having similar issues, it made sense to address these issues with the entire class. For example, if children were arguing at tetherball, four square, or another game on the playground, I often discovered that lots of problems occurred because there was not an agreed-on set of rules for the game. Having the class involved in solving the problem was helpful because many were perceptive enough to understand which parts of the game were causing conflict or confusion. When you include children in the actual solutions to a problem, they begin to recognize that they have the power and ability to problem solve.

It would be ideal to hold class meetings once per month. Class meetings had their own set of routines. The desks or chairs were moved into a circle so every child could make eye contact with each other. There was an agenda with the things I wanted to discuss, but the kids could also suggest topics for discussion. A portion of the meeting was devoted to recognizing good things that had been going on. Next, to the problem sheets, I had another stack of half sheet papers for something I called "The Friendship Club." (See Appendix) That was a place where kids could write a positive note about another student's actions that helped him/her. Over the years I discovered that spreading good news can be just as contagious as tattling, depending on the environment the teacher has helped to create. The Friendship Club gave students an opportunity to point out outstanding behavior around the school. This resource helped recognize some of those kids who needed a compliment the most. If a student had handled a problem appropriately, I might make mention of this. If students, who hadn't been doing their homework, had significantly improved, I would tell the class about this. Many times, I had the kids clap for one another for many types of accomplishments. I saw class meetings as a time to deal with problems, but it was also a time to celebrate individual or class achievements. I mentioned before that I liked to have some privilege that the class was working toward, and this would be an excellent time to get their input regarding future goals.

Working with Parents

As teachers, we are not only in the education business, but we are in the public relations business as well. There are times when some of the employees in a school fail to recognize this. Often, neighboring schools, in effect, compete for the same kids. I learned early in my career that it makes it easier when the parents are involved and support their child's school and teacher. Administrators and teachers help determine the level of involvement they want with parents, but skilled educators know how important families are to the children's success. Every effort should be made to keep parents informed and to provide them with opportunities that contribute to the betterment of the school.

When I first started teaching, my primary focus was on my students, as it should be; however, over time, it became clear that building positive relationships with parents was also a critical component. By establishing these relationships early in the year, you are more likely to have their support when you need it.

To start each year off on the right foot with your students and parents, get to know the incoming kids. After I received my new class list, I studied my yearbook from the prior year so that I could address the students by name when they first came into my classroom. Before the start of each school year, I inevitably received visits from parents bringing their child to meet me. With the nerves that come with having a new teacher, parents and teachers can assist children in adjusting to an unfamiliar situation. It was also the parents' opportunity to check the new teacher out as well. I was ready for them, and this was the time to make a good first impression. As they walked into the room for the first time, I addressed the child by name. A beaming face from a child or parent was often the result. I might even add a short anecdote of how I remembered the child by saying something like, "I remember that you are good friends with Miguel. He was in my class last year, and I used to see you guys playing basketball at recess."

It means a lot to the parents and child when you already recognize your new student and you are developing a healthy connection. You are building trust with a parent, and that is always a good thing. The parents or child sometimes responded by telling me that he/she was hoping to be in my room. With this simple act, you have made everyone (including yourself) feel more at ease. If you teach at a school for many years, you are bound to start teaching younger siblings of previous students. What teacher doesn't like hearing that parents requested you to be their child's teacher because one of their other children had such a good learning experience with you in a prior year?

Send parents a welcome letter to introduce yourself and provide them with information on how to make contact with you in the event that they may want to reach out to you. One of my fellow teachers used to make up refrigerator magnets with her contact information to give to the parents. It's a good idea to provide parents with several ways of reaching you because everyone's situation is different. There were plenty of working parents whom I rarely saw unless I happened to be at school when they were picking their child up from the after-school program. Some parents feel nervous or socially awkward when approaching the teacher. Providing e-mail or phone information offers an alternative means to make contact if they are uncomfortable or unable to do so in person. At the very least, give out the school phone number and your work e-mail. I also gave out my home phone number, but I certainly can understand why some people would not be comfortable doing this. My name was in the phone book for my entire career, so I never felt the need to make it private. When I did give my phone number to parents, I requested that they not call past a specific time. No one ever abused this privilege, and you will probably find that most parents will either contact you via e-mail or reach out to you at school anyway To be on the safe side, it is probably wiser just to give out the school phone number and school e-mail rather than anything personal. Sometimes I would be with a colleague after work, and they would get a text message from a parent. They were comfortable with this. I never texted with parents, but some of my colleagues stayed in contact with parents this way.

Keeping parents informed is crucial, so they know what their children are learning, and they are aware of what has been going on at school. Contact between a teacher and a parent should happen as soon as an issue arises, not halfway through the year after the child has been repeatedly disrespectful or weeks have passed without homework completion. Talk to parents before school, after school, over the phone, and by e-mail to stay in close touch. I sent a weekly report (See Appendix) each Monday that kept parents apprised of what we had studied the previous week and what was in store for the week ahead. The weekly report also provided information about what days the child finished his/her homework on time and how well the child behaved the previous week. I sometimes wrote a personal note on the report if I wanted the parent(s) to know something specific about their child. The kids were to return the weekly report in two days with a parent's or guardian's signature. These reports took about three hours to complete most weeks. (I usually worked on them after school on Friday or came in to work on a Saturday so that they would be ready to be taken home on Monday by the kids.) While they could be time-consuming, I always got so much positive feedback from the parents. They would tell me how much they appreciated the notes and felt that they had a much better understanding of what was going on with their child. This feedback was helpful as teachers are always forced to make choices on how best to utilize their time because there is still so much to do outside of regular class time.

I preferred contact with people in person, if possible, but this wasn't always practical for parents. Meeting face to face seemed to decrease any miscommunication. When reading an e-mail or text, you miss the subtleties that body language and tone of voice can provide. E-mail certainly has its advantages because parents can use it when it is most convenient for them. I had parents who worked during the day and had to reach me in the early morning hours or after dinner. Responding to a question or concern via e-mail gave me the time needed to carefully craft my thoughts and ensure that the response was clear and professional, before hitting send.

I know that some of my colleagues tried to maintain a class website during the year, and this was an effective way for parents to get information at a time that was convenient for them. After receiving parental permission to post photos on the Internet, one colleague often made slideshows of things that were happening in his class and put them on his class website. What a fabulous way to let grandparents and other relatives, who may not live locally, know what is happening in your class!

I got a lot of positive feedback from the parents by merely trying to keep them informed about what was going on in my classroom. I think the number one complaint that I heard parents voice over the years was the concern that some teachers or the school, in general, did not communicate well enough with them.

Being both a teacher and a parent with a son who attended the same school gave me a different perspective in regards to communication. My wife and I were happy with every teacher our son had in elementary school, but there were some years when we received very little information about what he was learning in school other than what he told us. Since I taught anywhere from grades 2-6, I had a pretty good idea what the grade level standards were. However, many parents won't have any idea what their child is learning unless you keep them informed.

Besides watching my child pass through our school, there were other times when I taught the children of some of my colleagues. One year I taught the son of a prominent county administrator, and I also had the privilege of educating the children of some of my fellow teachers from our school. These were somewhat unique situations, but I treated their children as I would any of my students. Most of the time these children were excellent students, but there were rare occasions when I just had to pass on observations that weren't very positive. Of course, if you ever find yourself in a situation like this, as with any parents, deliver the observations tactfully, sensitively, and share them only with the parents or guardians.

One year when I was teaching 6th grade, I had a substitute teacher who also happened to be the parent of one of my students. After I returned from a conference, some kids in my class accused the substitute of showing favoritism toward her child. While I doubt this was the case, it made for a difficult situation. Never subject a student in your class to these kinds of baseless accusations. Sometimes teachers' children attended our school in another colleague's classroom. At times other adults reported incidents to the parent/teacher in a more public setting like the staff room. Although probably not done to embarrass the parent/teacher, I could see how this was awkward for colleagues. At one point I could have taught my son when he passed through second grade, but my wife and I decided that it would probably be easier on him and me if we just avoided this situation altogether, and we put him in another teacher's classroom.

I would estimate that far more than half of the parental contacts I initiated were of a positive nature. That could be anything from a compliment over an act of kindness I witnessed, an academic success, improvement in concentration, a positive change in work habits, or just about any other excellent quality that deserved recognition.

Parents received copies of my homework and discipline policies at the start of the year so that they would understand my expectations. I frequently used the guidance of Lee Canter, a former teacher, and author of several books on assertive discipline, to assist me when I was typing up these policies. I'll never forget one parent who wrote back saying, "Now that I know what your expectations are, I want you to know what my expectations are of you." She proceeded to tell me that it was my responsibility to teach her child and that she would not require him to do any homework. She also wanted me to know that she would not be helping her child with anything academic because "that is your job." That parent sent the tone for our relationship, and I virtually had no contact with her for the entire year because she didn't come to any parent-teacher conferences or other school events. When her son acted up in class, I realized that I wasn't going to get any support from her, and I did the best I could under the circumstances. It is through no fault of the child when they are being raised by a parent who doesn't know how to be a parent. Good parenting requires love and discipline, and if either is missing, the chances of raising a happy and independent child are slim.

The majority of your students' parents will be great, but there were rare occasions when parents did something rather presumptuous or downright rude. Parents were supposed to go through the office at our school when trying to pull a child out for an appointment and not go directly to the child's classroom. It is easy to comprehend why such a policy was in place. If a parent pulled out a child by going directly to your room instead of through the office, then the school secretary wouldn't even be aware that a child was no longer on campus. There were rare occasions when one parent might violate a custody agreement and show up to take the child out of school. If somebody who isn't on the emergency card wants to pick up the child, the school should not be releasing the child to this individual. If the school doesn't make contact with the parent, then the proper protocol of reaching out to the people listed on the emergency card must be followed.

One specific memorable experience occurred when a parent walked into our classroom unannounced five minutes before the end of a school day with birthday invitations. Never mind that I was trying to get my students packed up and cleaned up before they left following an art project! The real issue was that it was a Friday, and the parent was trying to give out invitations to a birthday party that was happening that weekend! I typically would have told her that

I'd pass out the invitations tomorrow in class, but this was impossible since the party was that weekend. There were no more school days between now and then. Should I penalize this child for having a disorganized parent and insist that she not pass out the invitations? I couldn't do it, but what ensued was a massive fiasco as I ended up with kids in tears because she "miscounted" and didn't have enough invitations for all of the kids. Meanwhile, there were probably other parents in the parking lot wondering why the teacher couldn't let his class out on time.

In thirty-one years, I had only a handful of occasions when a parent came at me in a verbally angry or threatening manner. One time I was working with a small group of kids after school in my classroom, and a parent came in and just berated me in front of my students. She felt like I was assigning too many big projects for homework. While I knew that I had done nothing wrong, incidents like this can be pretty upsetting, especially to a young teacher. As I gained more experience, I learned not to take this sort of thing so personally, and thankfully they didn't happen often. Some people are just plain miserable and take out their frustrations on anyone in their path. Of course, it is a lot easier if you can get along with everybody, but the reality is that not every person you deal with will act in rational ways. This particular case was strange because, over the years, I had more parents who thought that I didn't give enough homework than too much.

The only other memory I have of a parent being indignant with me was an incident involving one of my third graders during the flag salute. Part of my philosophy as a teacher and as a parent was that it was important to give my students jobs that helped teach them something about responsibility and leadership. Most years I had the kids rotate through and do one of the many tasks that helped keep our classroom running smoothly. Jobs included sharpening the pencils, passing out the papers, bringing the lunch count attendance to the office, taking care of the class pets, acting as the class messenger (whenever I needed a student to get a supply or bring a note to a fellow teacher), or just about any other job with which I thought the kids could help.

One of the regular jobs was the flag salute leader. The student's role was to hold up the flag. The student would then make sure everyone was standing and ready, then lead the class in the Pledge of Allegiance while the other kids put their hand on their heart or saluted the flag. None of the class jobs were required, but typically everyone participated. If students didn't want to do a job, then they could pass on it, but most children were thrilled to have a classroom job. The kids did their class jobs for a week, and then the following Monday new students would fill the roles. Some children did not salute the flag because of religious beliefs, and I understood and respected this right. The kids who did not want to participate merely stood during the flag salute, and it was up to the kids if they chose to salute the flag or say the pledge. I used this same process for years and never had a parent complaint until one weekend I got an e-mail from a parent who was very upset with me.

It seemed that one Sunday, she and her family were talking about the flag salute in their home. Her daughter had been the flag salute leader about two months prior. The daughter had told her mom that I had forbidden her to say "amen" at the end of the pledge. The mother was furious with me for "shaming her daughter" over this alleged incident and felt that her daughter should be able to say "amen" without my censorship. The problem was that at no time did I ever forbid her child, or any other child for that matter, from saying this. To be honest, I have no recollection of any student of mine ever having said "amen" at the end of the pledge. When it comes to politics and religion, I have always found that these two topics are hot-button items for some people, and I tend to keep my opinions to myself. In fact, if anything, I always tried to avoid taking a public stance on these kinds of personal issues because I did not look to start disagreements or try to convince other people that I held the "correct" position on such individual preferences. In this particular situation, I had always found her daughter to be an honest girl. To this day I just believe that she simply misunderstood something I said or did in class. Over the course of the next couple of days the parent calmed down, but before that, she was threatening to pull her children from the school because of my alleged comments.

There were also times when kids came in upset about something that happened on the playground, and I asked them why they were arguing. In 2nd or 3rd grade, these arguments/disagreements might suddenly put me on the spot of trying to mediate a dispute between kids regarding their beliefs. I can recall a time when kids came in from recess quite agitated and asked me, "Is there a Santa Claus? 'Monica' says it's all fake." Another difficult one was, "Jerry says I'm going to hell because I don't go to church." When a situation like this happened, I usually fell into full retreat mode. There was no way I could address this potentially controversial situation without offending somebody. I said something like, "I can't tell you what to think because not everybody agrees. I think you should talk to your mom and dad because it's not my place to tell you what to believe." Another normal response from me when something was controversial was to say, "We're not going to talk about this." I am not exaggerating; things like this did happen from time to time.

Often the first contact with most of your parents will be on Back to School Night. Even by the end of my career, I felt some nervousness and anxiety about this night. I don't know why this was so because my colleagues told me many times that I was an excellent public speaker. I guess it just had to do with wanting to create a positive first impression and the fact that I was speaking in front of parents instead of children. Somehow having all of those adult eyes on me at once was a bit unnerving. After my presentation there usually was time for a brief question-and-answer period. Sometimes there were no questions, which in itself could be a little awkward. If there were no questions, I would make a joke of how well I must have explained things to them. I tried many things over the years to make myself less nervous about this event, but realized that there was no way to avoid these normal feelings. Some years I made an agenda of what I wanted to go over with the parents so that I would have a guide to help keep me on track. Most years I made a handout for the parents that covered the things I wanted them to know. Some teachers liked to create PowerPoint programs or used other types of technology to make their presentation to the families. One benefit of this was that it could be prepared ahead of time and gave a teacher a better way to control the pace of the presentation. It also took away the pressure of having so many eyeballs focused on you.

One year I moved all the desks into a circle and sat with the rest of the parents while I was talking to them. At my school, we usually had a twenty-minute presentation, with a five-minute passing period, followed by another twenty-minute presentation. The reason for making two presentations was because many parents would have more than one child who attended the school. That would give them an opportunity to visit both classrooms. One of the things that were always awkward for me (I'm sure this also happened to some of my colleagues too), was that after the first presentation, a lot of parents would want to come up and introduce themselves and ask how their child was doing so far. Meanwhile, the second group of parents had come in and was expecting you to start before the first group of stragglers left. When this happened, I made some kind of joke of "not wanting to keep the parents there all night" if the first group didn't pick up on the vibe that I needed to start with the next group.

I seemed to be a lot more comfortable during Open House which typically was held late in the school year. Open House was a time when the parents could come to school with their children to see their children's schoolwork and projects. I didn't have to make any formal presentation, knew most of the parents pretty well at that point, and I was pretty good at these kinds of situations because I could just be myself. I often tried to get a family photograph of my students with their relatives strategically placed around one of their projects. I didn't start using this idea until the last few years of my career, but most parents and kids enjoyed this, and it helped everybody relax. I often tried to use some of these photos in the end-of-the-year CD that

I made for my students. I think the thing that probably made me most uncomfortable on nights like this was having to dress up. I avoid ties if at all possible, and while I usually came to work wearing a dress shirt and pants, I was more comfortable when I could be more casual. I was the guy who ran around playing dodgeball with his class at P.E., and if I got a little sweaty in the process, so be it.

One thing to think about ahead of time is how you feel about having parent volunteers in your class. If you are a new teacher, perhaps you have no idea. I always had parent volunteers in my class. I worked with other teachers who never wanted volunteers. I found having volunteers to be particularly helpful, and parents contributed in so many different ways. I sent a parent volunteer list home by the second week of school with a list of jobs for which the parents could sign up. I liked to have a volunteer database readily available when I needed help. I used parents to correct papers, put up new bulletin boards, read with or work with children on a skill, help with typing and computer projects, run off papers for future lessons, manage my classroom book orders, attend field trips as chaperones, plan class parties, or whatever else I could think of for them to do. One of the things I liked to do was to have a cooking project occasionally. On days like this, it was beneficial to have volunteers who could help with the project or take photographs. One of my favorite annual projects was to cook a whole meal with my class. If you are going to take on something this ambitious, then you need to have a lot of parent volunteers who are willing to run a center. I almost always had working parents who wanted to help out in some capacity but had a hard time attending because of their job. However, if I let the parents know ahead of time about days like this, then some would get the day off. Some of my working parents also helped by correcting papers at home or buying snacks for the class.

Most parent volunteers I had were very helpful, but not every experience turned out great. I wanted parents to help out in my class as long as having them there didn't create other distractions. One of the things that you may find out is that the parent's child may act differently when the parent is there to volunteer. That could vary from a child behaving more positively than usual, or the other extreme of the child acting helpless and want the parent to give him/her unnecessary attention.

The kids and volunteers have to know your expectations when you have parents or other visitors in the classroom. For example, the kids were trained to address adults with a title of respect such as Mr., Mrs., or Miss. I have had adults who decided that they wanted the kids to refer to them by a first name. In some cases, the kids typically do this outside of school with that person already. The last thing you want to see is the creation of separate kinds of acceptable behaviors you wouldn't usually approve of when you are the only adult in the classroom. If you allow this to happen, younger students will feel the need to get out of their seats and hug these guests when they enter the room. As much as that might be a sweet thing, I didn't allow that to happen because during a regular school day people are coming and going all the time. Similarly, you don't say goodbye to students who are about to use the bathroom or greet them when they return to class after a trip to the office, and you don't want guests to interrupt the learning that is taking place in your classroom. I worked with a popular music teacher who used to pop his head in on occasion. It was always good to see him, and if the class hadn't started yet, a lot of the kids and I might even go over and hug him. The kids need to know that there are appropriate times for these kinds of things.

As a long-time teacher, I never got nervous in front of children. On the other hand, it is normal to feel a little nervous when you have a new parent volunteer working in your room for the first time. After I had developed a rapport and trust with parents, this quickly subsided. With new parent volunteers, I usually asked them to perform a simple task or invited them in for a short period. Even though I had confidence in my abilities as a teacher, it was human nature to feel a little nervousness when I was speaking in front of my peers. After establishing trust, they were just another helpful person in the room.

It is important to be discreet and professional around parent volunteers. Sometimes they want to gossip about other children or families in the class. Even if this occurs at a time when no other children are in the room, it is entirely inappropriate and unprofessional to engage in conversations of this type. You have to be clear (check with your administrator) about what your parent volunteers are allowed to do. If they are working with individual students, it is most likely that the volunteers need to be in the room with you (as opposed to going to another space). Regular parent volunteers (a sad and unfortunate reality) are fingerprinted to ensure that they are not registered sex offenders or felons.

It is important to realize that while you become quite friendly with many of the parents in a community over the years, you also have to remain professional in your dealings with them. In other words, it would not be appropriate to date a parent or go out drinking with him/her. You can't and shouldn't be talking about other children to parents. Sometimes parents will try to engage you in such conversations, and they may undoubtedly have a problem with one of your other students. On occasion, I had parents tell me something like, "I don't want 'Mary' sitting next to my child in the room. We have had nothing but problems with her in the past." If a parent made this kind of request, I often tried to accommodate it. At the same time, the parent should understand that you can't control every minute of every school day. It could be awkward when I felt like their child was the more significant problem than the student they were complaining about, but my philosophy as a teacher was always to choose my battles carefully. I listened to parental requests and considered them, but at times I just had to tell the parent what I'd observed, even if it didn't paint their child in the best light. If a parent requests a meeting, view this as an opportunity to work together to help the student. Try to set up a time that works well for both of you. I liked to meet with parents after school. Meeting before school does not allow enough time to get ready for the school day, and if a meeting does not go particularly well, it can disrupt the flow of the entire day.

Many parents enjoy coming to school on field trip days to

accompany the class. I liked having a few parents along to serve as chaperones when we were taking a field trip. On one particular field trip, we visited a nearby marsh to check out the local wildlife that we had been learning about in class. After stopping at a nearby park for lunch, we were supposed to go swimming for an hour at the local pool. In the real live teaching world, you have to deal with unforeseen problems. Most parents who went along with the class were just content to watch and chaperone the kids, but some parents asked if they could go swimming as well. I had taken this field trip about five times previously, and so I anticipated this situation. I didn't have any issue with it, and we had never had any problems in the past.

On this particular occasion, one of the parents from the other teacher's classroom came out of the dressing room wearing his swimsuit and carrying a towel. That was not unusual at all, but what was different was that he was wearing an ankle bracelet. I was teaching 2nd grade at the time, and I imagine that a lot of my students didn't understand the circumstances or were even aware that he had this on. After we listened to the pool rules from the lifeguard, the kids were excited and ready to get in the water. This unexpected twist threw my teaching colleague for a loop, and she came over to me and asked what we were going to do about this. I assumed he was on probation that required him to wear this, but I know how uncomfortable we both felt as he walked into the pool area. My colleague was probably as surprised as I, and she asked me to go over and talk to him. I imagine she felt a little troubled by the whole situation as did some of the other parents who were accompanying us. Fortunately, after I spoke to him, the guy decided not to make an issue or cause a confrontation. He left without incident, but it was very uncomfortable and awkward.

On another 2nd-grade field trip, I had a child who became angry and bit another student so forcefully that the bite broke the skin. This type of behavior from a 2nd grader was uncharacteristic for most students this age. I felt it was grounds to have the child sent home, and I had to call the grandparent on my cell phone. Unfortunately, we were at a park about forty-five minutes from school, and there was no other option except to have the grandparent (legal guardian of the child) come to get the student. To make matters worse, she didn't leave right away and then couldn't find the park for quite some time. My class was boarding the bus to go back to school when she arrived. She seemed annoyed at me about having to come to pick up her grandchild, but I knew that I had made the right call in this case.

Many kids at our school attended the after-school program, as the parents took advantage of this low cost or free service. Having so many kids attending provided me with extra opportunities to work with individual or small groups of children. Parents appreciated it and most elementary school-aged children thought this was fun. I would contact parents and work with them to develop a schedule so I would have some time to work with their child after school. Making contact with the parents in advance ensures that children aren't picked up early on the days you can work with them. Be aware that some older children may feel a little self-conscious or think that they aren't smart when you offer to tutor them. Perhaps sharing a story from your youth about a time when somebody helped you at school might make the child feel less self-conscious.

Anytime you witness a drastic change in a child's behavior or performance, reach out to parents, whether the changes are positive or negative. It's easy to contact parents to spread some good news, but sometimes teachers are guilty of forgetting to do this. That can be true of the kids who consistently make good choices and have good work habits already. It is natural to invest a lot of time trying to rectify problems, but it is so important to recognize those students who do the right thing each day as well. When you observe positive changes in behavior or academics, it may seem evident to praise your student. Another obvious step is to make positive contact with a parent/guardian when these changes occur. That should take place in the form of personal contact at school, e-mail, or by sending a note home. Sometimes I would call a parent with the child in my presence and would often put the child on the phone for a minute. Talk about immediate reinforcement! When he/she would hang up the phone, there was usually a broad grin on the student's face.

The more challenging contacts are equally necessary. Good teachers should not avoid contact with a parent because they fear what the parent's reaction will be. Does a doctor only call patients when there is good news? Of course not! You are just doing your job when you show your concern for a child who is misbehaving or exhibiting poor work habits. If I observed some new negative behavior in a student that I hadn't seen before, I became quite concerned. Sometimes there was a logical explanation for their anger, irritability, sleepiness, or disrespect. Many elementary children are entirely forthcoming with things that are going on in their lives, but not always. How could a child not be upset if a pet has just died, a close family member has just gone to the hospital, or if parents are speaking about getting divorced? These things all happened at one time or another during my career. Sometimes parents will give a heads up, but at other times it is only discovered when a child begins to cry for no apparent reason.

You can't make contact for every single incident that happens at school, or you will spend the majority of your day on the telephone. The general rule of thumb I made for myself about whether or not to contact a parent: Would I want to know about this if I were the child's parent? I think that this is just common sense, but developing guidelines in advance regarding when to contact a parent is proper planning.

When things aren't going well educationally or socially for a child, it is important to offer your support and to work with the parents as needed. I generally felt supported by parents and felt like their responses were appropriate when I contacted them. There were, however, times that I was blown away by a parent's lack of concern. For example, if I had a student who took someone else's property, I would want to know about this if I were the child's parent. Most saw this as important, but I had some adults who tried to make excuses for their child. I've had parents tell me on occasion, "Well, that's only because someone in your class took his property," or, "Well, she sees her friends with new school supplies, and we can't afford that. I'm not really surprised that she took it." Or despite the fact that the child has been caught red-handed, "My child knows better than that. He would never take someone's book!" It is hard to reason with parents that make excuses for their children and not take it personally if an adult tries to blame you for their child's behavior. "Well, he didn't do this last year in Mrs. Smith's class." (As if you are the sole reason why their child has become a thief.) These responses put a teacher in a difficult position. Instead of defending yourself as one may naturally want to do, you have to remain in control of your emotions. A mature response would be to offer your own solution. "Well, I'm sorry you feel that way, but I really want to work with you in helping 'Johnny.' I'm concerned about him, but I have an idea that I think might help. First of all, I do think he needs to write a letter of apology to 'Stan'. I'll help him write the letter at recess tomorrow if he doesn't know what to say. After that, I'd like to talk to him about finding a more positive way that he earn a book. I have some jobs that he can help me do in my classroom. If we can teach him that he can earn things through hard work instead of taking things that don't belong to him, I think this will be a valuable lesson for him to learn."

There was no guarantee that this kind of approach would work for that parent/child, but to me, it was worth the investment. Not only are you helping the child learn right from wrong, but you may also be showing a parent an idea that he/she had never thought of before. As one of my oldest teacher friends always used to say to me, "Just because you're a parent doesn't mean you know how to be a parent."

I went out of my way to make conversation with parents in other environments. If I saw a parent in the grocery store, I said hi and asked them about their child. If a parent owned a business, then I might try to frequent it. I once knew a parent who was the owner/manager of a local restaurant. On occasion, I would bring in my wife, mom, or a friend for dinner at his establishment. Over the years I developed a very positive relationship with this man, and he would tell my dining companions that I was one of the best teachers his kids ever had.

He often supplied all of the food for our parent-teacher organization when it came to holding our annual pancake breakfast. Developing a positive reputation throughout the parent community can only help you in the long run.

One of the most critical times to communicate with parents is when you are holding a parent-teacher conference. Having done a lot of conferences over the years, I have some advice on the best way to conduct these meetings. The attitude that you present toward the parents is going to have a lot to do with how successful and meaningful each parent conference is. My first thought is that the parent needs to see the two of you as being on the same team rather than rivals. The ultimate goal of doing whatever is best for the child should be the common bond that you both share. I felt like I failed as a teacher if the parent viewed me as an adversary rather than a caring and dedicated teacher. Presenting unpleasant surprises to a parent is the worst way to go about a conference. You should be communicating with the parent at times throughout the year and not just at conferences. If a child has been doing poorly with his/her schoolwork, hasn't been doing homework, or has been being argumentative and disrespectful to adults around the school, the conference shouldn't be the first time the parent hears this.

Conferences will go better when you keep the parents abreast throughout the trimester/quarter, even if the report isn't favorable. I started each conference describing some of the strengths of each student. If a student was belligerent, disrespectful, or struggled academically, I could always find some positive qualities to recognize. Telling a parent that their child is hard working (even if he/she struggles in school), kind, respectful, follows the rules, works well with others, or participates a lot in class are positive attributes.

I liked to divide the conferences into two main parts. The first part was to talk about and show examples of what the child was doing well in school. The second part of the conference was examining those areas in which the child could use some support, and I would suggest ideas. I left a few minutes for both parent and child to share any concerns they might be having. There were times when the parent or child might bring up a previous incident that occurred; sometimes I was aware of these things, but not always.

When you report that a child is struggling in a particular area, you need to be able to tell the parent what steps you have already taken or what you intend to try in the future. Most parents rightly view you as the professional, and they are looking for ideas. If you report negative things, but don't have any suggestions on how to help the child, then are you a person who takes his job seriously? Are you getting the child some tutoring? Are you guiding parents to make them aware of unfamiliar resources? What are you willing to do to help your student? Many times the parents are looking for support, and as a professional, you should be able to provide different avenues of help.

Be honest, but tactful, in your parent-teacher conferences. Some parents get defensive if they think you are judging them. I often shared my own experiences as a parent if I thought it applied to the situation. Sometimes parents need to hear we all face struggles when we are trying to raise children, including the teacher.

You meet all types of parents at conferences. Most were kind and friendly, but I also dealt with hostile parents. When I could feel a parent was nervous at the beginning of a conference, I tried to tell them a funny anecdote about their child to lighten the mood. Sometimes I'd been forewarned by other teachers about a particularly challenging parent, but at other times a parent would come in angry about an issue of which I wasn't even aware. On occasion, I had no inkling why the parents seemed to have a negative attitude. These conferences were challenging because I didn't know at first if the parent was angry at me, the school, having a personal problem, or just had a negative view on schools, in general, based on prior experiences. Even the most conscientious teacher won't always know about their students' problems in other areas on the school campus. I can recall learning for the first time at conferences that a parent was angry with a playground supervisor or after-school teacher regarding some prior incident.

One of the more common things that may arise during a conference is that a parent will tell you about having had similar academic or behavior issues when he/she was a child. While acknowledging that kids sometimes inherit personality traits and skills from their parents, don't accept that the same must be true for their children. If a parent admitted to not liking school as a child, don't fall into the assumption that things have to be the same way for their child. Many times, when I was talking to a parent about trying to get some tutoring for their child, I would hear a parent say something like, "Well, I wasn't good at math either." That may be true, but does that mean we shouldn't try to help their child to do better? It would be like us accepting the parent's excuse, "Well, I used to shoplift when I was a teenager too," as if this somehow makes their child's theft issues in your classroom acceptable.

Our school secretary scheduled most parent-teacher conferences after school, but sometimes you have to plan conferences before school or do them over the phone. We tried to accommodate those parents who had more than one child attending the school by scheduling the conferences consecutively on the same day. Conferences at our school lasted twenty minutes with a five-minute transition time between conferences. Of course, some sessions are likely to be shorter or longer. If you suspect a conference might take an inordinate amount of time, ask the secretary to schedule it as the last conference for the day so that other conferences will not be affected. If parents arrived late for the conference, leaving inadequate time to meet, I would try to reschedule the conference so as not to impact the following meetings. It isn't fair to inconvenience other families because another parent shows up late for his/her conference. Most people are reasonable about rescheduling their conference to another time.

Difficulty can occur when having a conference with biological parents who don't get along. Many divorced couples maintained a healthy relationship and were civil to one another when discussing what was best for their child. However, divorced couples may need separate conferences if they can't be in the same room with their former spouse without fireworks. It is quite likely that you may not be privy to these dynamics initially, but the secretary might possess more knowledge and schedule the conference accordingly.

The idea of holding separate conferences for dual sets of parents usually was a good strategy, but I also experienced frustration when the parent wanted to spend the time badmouthing the former spouse rather than discussing their child's progress. These conferences were probably the most frustrating for me because I had to remind the parent that we were there to discuss the child's academic progress and social growth.

Whether to include students at the conference was typically left up to the parents; however, I liked to have them in attendance. This way everyone was on the same page, and the child couldn't tell the parent one thing, while the teacher said something else. That also was an excellent way to delve into any concerns the parent or child had. There can be times when either the parent or you need to share some pertinent information without the child's presence, and in situations such as this, I just asked the child to step outside for a minute.

Some parent(s) will bring in very young toddlers with them. This can be distracting because parents often lose focus because they are concerned about what the child is doing. If I knew ahead of time that a toddler would likely be there, I tried to have a few things ready that the youngster could do (color, easy jigsaw puzzles, or even some simple manipulatives to keep the children occupied). I had conferences where a young child started taking things off the shelves as fast as his hands could manage. I've been shocked when a parent said nothing as the child reorganized, rearranged, and made a mess of my book or game shelves. In situations like this, I had to tell the parent that their child could not take my room apart. Of course, it is much better if the parent doesn't bring in a small child in the first place, but some circumstances are hard to control.

Parent-teacher conferences were held twice a year, but I let parents know I would be glad to meet with them at a time that would work for both of us at any point during the school year. Of course, I kept in contact in other ways throughout the year, as mentioned previously.

I have one more suggestion about the scheduling of parent conferences. We could tell the secretary when we did not want to do conferences so that she could accommodate our schedules too. The first conferences were scheduled to begin ten minutes after school ended. Part of our duties included waiting for those kids who were going home right after school to be picked up by a parent. If any arrived late, then I had no time to catch my breath before starting a succession of five or more conferences in a row. Even if you are incredibly organized, it takes time to gather everything you want to share at a conference. My advice is not to schedule a meeting in the first time-period slot because this will give you time to go to the bathroom, get organized, and relax for a few minutes before the first parent arrives. It does mean that you might have to stay at school a little longer that day, but for me, it was worth the trade-off.

Some parents don't realize how much teachers care about their students. I often felt as if my students were like my children. I felt proud when they did something well and disappointed when they made mistakes. When you run into former students' parents in the community, make the time to ask how their children are doing now. I was always interested to know what former students were up to years later, and your curiosity is a sign to the parent that teaching is more than just a job for you.

Working with Colleagues

One of the blessings of being a teacher is working with so many terrific, dedicated people. The majority of teachers are incredibly giving people who put in countless hours behind the scenes without the knowledge of most. After the school year gets into full swing, you may feel like a hamster in a wheel. It didn't matter how fast I'd run; that wheel kept spinning. As one of my longtime colleagues used to say, "After the first day, you never feel like you're caught up." There is always something to do. Can you be a teacher and put in only the minimum amount of work while giving a half-hearted effort? I suppose you can, but very few people I worked with ever approached teaching in that way. As with any profession, there are going to be those who either aren't as skilled at their craft or don't have the passion and love for teaching that most teachers possess. In my experience, this was the exception, not the rule.

I advise any teacher entering the profession to understand that education works best when you view yourself as part of a team. You need to do your best as an individual, but also must encourage teamwork and cooperation with the entire staff. The administration can help promote this type of working environment among staff, but it also requires the commitment of each staff member. I worked with teachers who were supportive teammates and others who purposefully kept to themselves. The best working environment is one in which your colleagues support and help one another. These partnerships form most closely among teachers who are teaching in the same grade, but a cohesive staff is one that works together across grade levels. If you all are using the same curriculum or using the same schoolwide discipline plan, then everyone should be empowered to be an integral part of the team.

Every teacher has good and bad teaching days. It comes with the territory. Some days things go off the rails for no apparent reason, and you question your career choice, while on other days everything goes so smoothly, and you feel like the best teacher in the world. Sometimes there are logical reasons why you have off days. Perhaps you are dealing with your family problems, and you aren't as patient as you usually are. Maybe you didn't get enough sleep, and you're just cranky that day.

Lots of times your students are going through difficult things that you may not be aware of that can affect their mood or dealings with other children. A child could be upset because a relative is in the hospital, one of their pets may have passed away, perhaps the child's parents are fighting, or the hundreds of other things that can happen to any of us to change our mood and affect how we are feeling about ourselves. Sometimes it is hard to reason why you suddenly have a terrible day from out of the blue. The longer you teach, the more you realize that this is the ebb and flow of a regular school year. Being able to talk to your colleagues openly about these moments is important because sometimes we need to rely on one another for support. I'm sure it is human nature for most teachers to want to project an aura of confidence to their students and the parents of their students. You want your students and parents to feel that they have an educator who knows how to handle and deal with just about any situation. We certainly would like the professionals in our lives to express this same confidence. Would you feel comfortable going to doctors, dentists, or lawyers who seemed unsure of themselves?

While we want to project confidence, I believe there isn't a teacher alive who hasn't occasionally had an off day. When this happens, it is nice to be able to confide in your colleagues about how you're feeling. If I told my co-workers about my students struggling with a particular lesson, I might find out that they had the same experience. It was reassuring to know that other teachers struggled with the same task, or perhaps, more importantly, had a suggestion of what they did to make the lesson more successful. Some children were challenging regardless of their teacher, but at times colleagues had insights or ideas about what worked for them.

I would recommend that grade level colleagues try to meet for a planning session at least one day per week. Some teachers plan together every day depending on the availability of fellow staff members. I felt it was nearly impossible to meet every day with my grade level colleagues because it regularly seemed like we had to be responsible for a multitude of other things before the next day of school. In a small school like ours, just about every teacher served on one or more committees which met regularly after school. Of course, things come up that are going to interfere with meeting regularly, such as medical or dental appointments, illnesses, jury duty, or dealing with your family matters. It is helpful in situations like these for someone to take notes to share with those unable to attend and to bring them up to speed. They might have something to offer that none of the group considered. Your colleagues deserve to know what you decided as a group. Having excellent communication skills with fellow staff members prevents problems with your co-workers.

All teachers seem to have those subjects that they are more knowledgeable in or find more interesting to teach. I believed that some of my stronger areas of teaching were math, writing, and physical education. Two areas that I wasn't as skilled in were teaching technology and art. Pride sometimes gets in the way of your learning and improving as teachers. Being able to acknowledge our strengths and weaknesses is a significant hurdle to overcome. Once again, you will often find among your fellow staff members that there are individuals who may be more knowledgeable than you are in specific areas of the curriculum. Even if you're an experienced teacher, there is always something to learn. I found it more efficient to get help from a colleague who could share his/her expertise rather than trying to discover something on my own. If you know that you are weaker in a particular area, look for opportunities to enhance your learning by seeking out members on the staff who can offer their support or consider signing up for classes that may improve your teaching.

You may possess strengths or expertise in areas of the curriculum in which some of your colleagues may be weaker. I always made time when asked for help, and this show of support benefited me when I, too, needed assistance. Sometimes a colleague and I would trade classes for a period. In my last year of teaching, one of my 3rd-grade colleagues asked me to take her class for physical education. I always loved P.E., and I enjoyed sharing my love for it with another set of kids. During this period, she took my kids for social studies, and I left the planning and teaching of that up to her. Switching classes gave the kids an opportunity to become accustomed to having more than one teacher. As children get older and move into middle school and high school, they have to get used to having several teachers with different styles in the same day.

On occasion, we experimented with having a student choice period once a month. Our students could sign up for the activity that most interested them. We offered activities to the kids in science, art, physical education, technology, music, or whatever subject/activity a teacher might want to teach. The kids in each of our grades would sign up in advance for the class that they wanted to attend. Some of the choices were more popular than others so that we would limit the number of children per activity. Since I allowed my students to choose what they wanted to do randomly, we usually ended up with some kids who did not get to sign up for their first choice. I kept track of the last five or six kids who were chosen and let them pick first the next time. Some teachers preferred not to take part in student choice days, and that was fine too. You will need to check in with your administrator to see how he/she feels about these classes. Most of my principals were very supportive, but some administrators preferred that we never divert from the standard curriculum.

Observing another teacher is a valuable way to learn how to

improve at implementing something. If the person you want to watch also happens to be in your school, most administrators will try to accommodate this. One way to facilitate this process was by having the principal take your class for a period while you observe your colleague. I also had principals that encouraged us to go to other schools and learn from other teachers. That became harder to do near the end of my career because we had a shortage of substitute teachers in our district.

When working with your colleagues, it is essential to keep an open mind since none of us have all the answers. If a colleague wanted to share something, I was always respectful to listen to suggestions. There is nothing more irritating than teachers who think they know everything and are unwilling to see somebody else's point of view. It may be that the idea will not work for you, but the input should be valued. If I found something useful that came from a fellow teacher, I would write a thank you note and let my principal know how helpful another colleague had been.

If you work in a larger school district, you will have several grade level colleagues. I once worked with two teachers who couldn't agree on much of anything. Some of their disagreements became quite opinionated. They were both talented teachers; it was just that their styles and the subjects they valued were different.

I'm a person who rarely finds himself in conflicts. I know that I can be hardheaded about certain things, but when it came to working together, I usually went along with the group consensus. Their particular set of dynamics was much harder because I felt like they were regularly trying to persuade me to adopt their position. I didn't always want to be the tiebreaker. It reminded me of times growing up when two of my friends were fighting, and they were asking me to take a side in their disagreement. I tried to stay out of these peer differences among staff members when they happened. The reality was they occurred quite infrequently. If asked to take a position on something important, such as what new curriculum our district should adopt, I stated my opinion and tried to support it with facts.

It is essential that you try to remain open-minded because someone else may offer input you hadn't even considered.

In addition to working with my grade level teachers, I often liked to find a teacher who taught at another level (two or more years apart) and team together to do some buddy lessons. It was worth the extra time to try to match students who were likely to work well together. Assigning partners at random, especially when working with a different grade level, wasn't a good strategy. For children with special needs, their partners should be mature to handle the situation better. The teacher of the younger grade usually comes up with the particular activity because the teacher of the older students may not know the specific areas of help needed. Once I found the right teaching partner, we might plan one of these cross-age tutoring periods every four to six weeks. Cross-age tutoring was a win/win arrangement. More often than not, the older children were good role models and provided support to their younger buddy. I witnessed situations where an older child, who may have traditionally been a behavior problem, rose to the occasion because many responded well when we placed them in the position of being a positive role model. The younger students also benefitted from this relationship. Not only were they getting some one-on-one help, but having a buddy made them feel safer and less intimidated by older students.

Occasional after-school gatherings are a great way to promote togetherness and friendships among teachers. It was fun to bring everybody together to go out to eat, having a BBQ, meeting for drinks, a movie, a play, or attending a sporting event. These activities are pretty easy events to throw together without a lot of effort. Try to include spouses, significant others, and children when you can.

Understand in advance that some people are not going to attend many of these social gatherings. All teachers have different responsibilities in their personal lives depending on the age of their children, and some teachers may not be able to participate in many of these things because of their family situations. Other people may feel like they haven't been able to spend much family time during the school week and preferred to spend time at home. As long as everyone understands that there is no pressure to participate, it's an enjoyable way to bring people together.

Developing healthy relationships with your colleagues means not engaging in gossip about others. Most teachers refrain from this type of behavior, but I witnessed this at times. Insecure people are usually the ones who feel the need to talk about others in a demeaning fashion, but I would advise not taking part in this unprofessional behavior. Would any of us want others discussing our inadequacies? It is not the responsibility of teachers to critique fellow staff members. It is quite likely that you'll be aware of many of the friendly peer relationships on staff, but chances are you won't know them all. It is only a matter of time before gossip gets back to another colleague, and then how will everybody feel? Negativity can damage the overall strength of a close staff.

It is quite common for teachers to talk about individual children that are challenging for them. I worked for one principal who felt this was inappropriate because she believed it was a confidentiality issue when we spoke about specific children. I didn't see it that way, but I always tried to respect the concept of privacy. Teachers are often looking for advice on how to deal with a difficult child. The problem was (this part I agree with my administrator about) that some of these conversations took place in a busy area like the staff room where people/parents come and go all the time. There are going to be times when you probably aren't even conscious of all the people in a staff room. In some cases, these might be new employees you haven't met yet, but they also might be the parents of the children who attend the school. If someone were there that I didn't know, I would introduce myself and find out who they were. Talking about something confidential when you don't even know all the people in the room is risky and unprofessional. It would be wiser to speak to a prior teacher privately to maintain confidentiality if you're looking for management strategies and other ideas.

In my district, we had a very close group of male teachers. We had our share of "boys' night out" gatherings, but what further brought this group closer was that many of us helped each other with home projects in the summer. When it came to painting a house, building a deck, putting up sheetrock, or taking off a roof, there was never a shortage of workers coming to the aid of another. I lacked the construction experience and talent that many of my co-workers had, but what I could offer was effort and a willingness to help. Many of us volunteered and jumped right in when it came to installing a new playground or other large projects within our district. I do think this was a unique situation, and our school district was lucky to have so many giving people who wouldn't think twice about giving up a Saturday for their students or school.

Most administrators and teachers I worked with treated every school employee with respect. I can't emphasize how important this is to the overall school climate. Every employee in the school has a hand in creating the environment in which you all work. I know that most people I have worked with respond better to a management style that values everyone on the staff for their contributions.

Many people on the support staff can go unrecognized or underappreciated for their efforts. We must not take for granted those staff members who are critical cogs in the success or failure within a school. The librarian, playground monitors, lunchroom monitors, bus drivers, custodians, and classroom aides are all critical personnel in setting the tone and environment for your school.

Not only that, but teachers are going to have some relationship with all of those people. Why not make it a positive one? I know that I tried to go out of my way to thank these employees for their efforts. Having a good working relationship with everyone in your school can only help you in the long run. When I witnessed someone doing their job well, I might mention this to the person directly or write a note to my boss to recognize these contributions. I knew my principal would take the time to pass on my comments to the employees too. I might see one of these people the following day, and they'd thank me for my words. Small gestures like giving a coffee card, a doughnut, a sandwich, or just showing your support for these people in front of the kids demonstrates you care for and value them. When you have a class party, there is almost always food left over. Instead of taking it home, try leaving something for the custodian who cleans your room daily or the secretary who does an endless variety of favors for you throughout the year. What you will often find is that these employees are seldom recognized and genuinely appreciate any special recognition you can give them. When the ladies in the cafeteria save you a treat from lunch or the custodian makes the extra effort to get something in your room fixed, it further reinforces why these relationships with the support staff at your school are so invaluable.

Working with Your Boss

I was fortunate to work with some outstanding administrators who were good at their jobs, genuinely cared about the students, and were passionate about education. If you teach for any length of time, it is likely that you will encounter excellent, average, and even poor administrators. At times I worked with friendly people who just weren't cut out to be principals/administrators, but it's always smart to maintain a friendly and professional relationship, regardless of whether they are good at the job. Many administrators were formerly teachers, and this is helpful since they are familiar with issues that come up during the course of a typical school year.

I was lucky to work with two outstanding principals, Cynthia Van Vleck and Nancy Wheeler, at the start of my career. They had been fantastic teachers in our district and mostly had the support of the staff when they became principals. Being a young teacher, I didn't fully appreciate the importance of a skilled principal until I had taught there for several years. Having a talented and supportive administrator is crucial to having a suitable environment in which to work.

A respected administrator sets the tone in your school. If the parents, teachers, other staff members, and children admire and look up to the principal, the working atmosphere will be much better. When I worked for someone I respected, it made me want to be the best teacher I could be. When we worked for an ineffective administrator, the overall morale was at its lowest. While I tried to remain professional and do my job when the parent community and fellow staff members were grumbling about the administration, it is hard not to let that affect your performance. I never felt that it was my role as a teacher to evaluate the administrator, and at no point did a school board member approach me and ask me whether or not I thought an administrator was doing a good job. Even If I didn't believe my boss was performing admirably, I never commented on this and just focused on doing everything I could to be an excellent teacher to my students. I wrote the school board a supportive letter about an administrator who I felt was doing an excellent job after encountering both fantastic and mediocre administrators. Do not take good administrators for granted when you are lucky enough to work for an inspiring leader. I had learned that outstanding administrators should not be taken for granted. While I never said a negative thing about any administrator to a parent, I definitely would share positive thoughts about a principal to the parent community in my weekly parent note. Many parents were very supportive of their child's teacher, and I felt it could only help when they knew that I valued a good administrator.

When establishing a relationship with any new administrator, I liked to determine whether our philosophies about education aligned with one another. A quality administrator in my book was one who had faith in the staff and took an active role in the education of the students in our school district. That included observing a leader who understood the importance of creating a safe environment for kids and demonstrated through his/her actions that the best interest of the students was always at the forefront of any decisions made.

A great communicator is a key to a quality administrator-one who can communicate effectively with the staff, kids, and parent community. Since local schools are competing with one another, having a well-respected principal and excellent teachers in a school are features that attract new families.

Some administrators were very much in the public eye and were out front greeting kids/parents daily and calling them each by name, and there were others who kept a much lower profile. From the perspective of a teacher and as a parent, I preferred principals and administrators who were friendly and outgoing with the community. We are asking parents to entrust their children's education and safety with us; shouldn't we be doing everything in our power to create a warm and safe environment?

Getting to know each child as soon as possible is a sign of a good principal. Maybe this isn't practical in a large school, but I felt that part of an administrator's job was to interact with the students in the school each day. How is a principal going to do that if he/she is sitting in the office all day long? Principals/Administrators have an obligation to make everyone feel welcome and cared for in the school. If administrators are going to be leaders in the school, it is imperative that they have a positive aura. Good administrators also make the extra effort to say a kind word to a child and to make every employee in the school feel valued. Those who are out front, active, and approachable are demonstrating the best form of public relations.

Award assemblies were held at the school to recognize students for some academic, attendance, or positive behavior accomplishment. Parents were often invited to attend these assemblies. These were opportunities to build trust within the community and to show parents that the teachers and other employees cared for their children. Typically, the awards assemblies demonstrated just that. On the other hand, I can recall situations when the administrator mispronounced some children's names when calling them up to receive their awards. Kids in the audience couldn't help themselves and would shout out to correct the principal's mispronunciation. When honoring students, what kind of message does this show the parent community when an administrator can't even pronounce the name of the students?

With new administrators, I was interested in learning how they handled discipline. I appreciated it when they took the time to explain their philosophy to the staff. Teachers and principals can vary in their approach when dealing with discipline. In most cases, I preferred to manage this on my own, so the kids would know that I was in charge of my classroom and could deal with any scenario. At the same time, there are situations when an uncooperative or disrespectful student needs to leave the room. On the rare occasion when I sent a child to the principal, I expected my administrator to support me and make sure that the child knew that neither of us was going to tolerate disrespect nor willful disobedience.

I think it is paramount to have the foresight to alert an administrator whenever something out of the ordinary happens with students or parents. For example, if a playground supervisor reported to me at the end of recess about a physical altercation that took place involving two of my students, then I would look into a serious matter such as this. I never assumed that the playground monitors would report the incident to the principal. After collecting some information, I would either send the involved parties to the office or at the very least, tell my administrator/principal about the scenario after school. It isn't fair to a principal/administrator to suddenly be thrust into a situation with an angry parent when the teacher could have forewarned him/her. Just as administrators have a responsibility to keep teachers in the information loop, administrators should expect the same.

There are going to be situations in which a misinformed parent either comes at you or your administrator with misguided anger. I recall one year when the teacher's union in our school district decided to have informational pickets on campus. We were meeting as a staff in front of the school before and after our normal hours to inform the public of relevant issues regarding our working conditions. That was out of the ordinary and was upsetting for everyone. I'm sure parents were questioning whether their child's teacher was about to go on strike. Older children probably wondered if their teacher would be coming to class that day. Some of our administrators presumably worried about the future and suddenly were facing the possibility of having to replace staff members should the teachers decide to hold a work stoppage. Many teachers, undoubtedly, felt anxious about the future and the repercussions, if any, such an action would have.

I was teaching 6th grade at the time, and my students kept asking me what was going on. I generally believe that it is better to speak openly and honestly about age-appropriate matters rather than to keep things from children. I knew my students would be curious, but I realized it wasn't my place to discuss our issues with them. I merely explained how sometimes people legally exercise their right to free speech in America. While I told my class that I couldn't go into the details, I informed them we were peacefully expressing our feelings and following the law. I left it at that, and I'm sure they still had a lot of questions, but I didn't feel it would be appropriate to involve them any further than this. One of my students' parents angrily called the school at the end of the school day and told the principal that I was propagandizing my students and involving them in school politics. I had a trusting relationship with my administrator, and she checked in with me to see what happened to cause this parent's reaction. After I explained the facts to the principal, she called the parent back, helped diffuse the situation, and went to bat for me by defending my integrity as a teacher to the parent. It was reassuring as a teacher to know that a principal wouldn't overreact and would look into a situation carefully before passing any judgment.

It has been my experience that most parents are reasonable and will support the teacher when they see that you are trying to help their child. When the situation warranted it, I called the parents to inform them and tell them why I was disciplining their child. Most of the time, the parents understood my position and supported me, but there were rare occasions when parents simply made excuses for the unruly behavior of their child. If I got off the phone and realized a parent was angry with me, I would go and speak to my principal about something like that. Sometimes a parent will go off verbally on you and threaten to "go to your boss" or "pull my child out of this school." I know my administrators would not want to get blindsided by an angry parent if the person decided to carry out their threat. By informing the administrator of the situation ahead of time, the principal/vice principal will understand the scenario and will be better prepared to address the matter if a parent came in all worked up. If, after we collaborated, a principal and I decided that a child was going to be disciplined, I checked with the administrator to see which one of us would be contacting the parent to inform him/her of what was going on. In most cases, this should be the principal's job at this point, but make sure that you are both on the same page.

Some days it can be difficult to make contact with the principal. You may go to the office several times during the day only to find that your boss is busy with students, parents, fellow employees, meetings, or numerous other things. It can be frustrating at times, but this is the reality. The principal might have to leave right after work and would be unavailable to talk about a matter that needed immediate attention. When this happened, and the situation called for prompt action, I would write my principal a letter that she could read first thing the next day, or I would send an e-mail that night. Most of my bosses would read the e-mail that evening and would either write me back then or make contact with me the following day.

One year we had kind of an unusual situation because our principal was at the other school site one day a week (on minimum days). A minimum day is one where the kids get out of school earlier than usual. Minimum days occurred for parent-teacher conferences, or they were in place for staff development. Most years that I was employed, the kids would get out an hour earlier than usual on Wednesdays. This particular year we had an acting principal on minimum days. I understood the importance of having someone be "in charge" when the administrator was gone, but in many cases, the acting principal was hardly qualified to do that job. One of the other problems was that there wasn't a consistent replacement. I remember once walking into the office and realizing the acting principal was a person who had only subbed for us on a couple of prior occasions. I couldn't help but laugh (to myself) at the ridiculousness of having an inexperienced substitute who was asking me fundamental teaching questions the day before and was now serving as "principal" the following day. Fortunately, that situation only lasted one year, and I never saw it again. Most of the time one of the other regular teachers at the school or the administrator at our sister school, South Bay, would be in charge when our principal attended a conference or was out with an illness. There should be a clear chain of command when an administrator is gone so that everyone is certain about who is in charge.

I know that sometimes one of my colleagues would go to the administrator and complain about another employee, but I would never do that unless I felt somebody's safety was at risk. I thought it was my job to worry about my students and myself rather than to critique the performance of others. Would I like it if one of my colleagues was going to my administrator to complain about something I was doing? Chances are there have already been complaints from parents or other personnel if an employee hasn't been doing a good job. I have had administrators come to me and ask me about someone who was working in my room. More often than not, the administrator was trying to find out if the employee was doing an adequate job. In this situation, I would answer my boss's question honestly, but I certainly felt it wasn't my place to comment on the abilities of my fellow teachers. I never was asked by an administrator about a fellow teacher's performance, but I don't think I'd offer an opinion unless I felt that the perception of an excellent teacher was misguided. There were only a couple of exceptions I would make to this rule. I would say something to either the person or the administrator if a student were placed in danger by the actions of a fellow teacher or supervisor.

One year a playground supervisor was allowing the kids to climb up on the walls for ball wall. A ball wall is a flat, wooden structure usually about six to eight feet in height in which a person can hit a ball against to act as a backboard. A ball wall is a necessity for the game of wall ball. Wall ball is usually played by two individuals who take turns attempting to strike a rubber ball with a closed fist. The object of the game is to make the ball hit twice before the opponent can reach it. To keep the game moving swiftly, the loser of a point goes out, and a new player comes in to face the winner of the previous point. Since the bigger kids could potentially climb and get atop the wall, this wasn't a safe thing for them to be doing. I felt it would only be a matter of time until one of the kids got hurt. I initially spoke to the supervisor and indicated that this was not something that he should be allowing the kids to do. I would have left it at that if this cured the problem, but the following week I saw the supervisors ignoring the same behavior. At that point, I went to my principal and mentioned what I had observed because it involved the safety of the children.

I also went to my principal to report a substitute teacher who was putting my class at risk. In this case, my students told me that the substitute had left them alone in the classroom for a considerable amount of time when she had gone to the bathroom. It is never appropriate to leave students unsupervised at school. If an emergency arose and I got sick or had to use the bathroom immediately, I would call the office and get someone to take my place for a few minutes. My third graders had never experienced a time when the teacher abruptly left, and they suddenly were unsupervised. They were bright enough to realize that this wasn't normal, and I'm glad they told me about it. I suppose there was some chance that the adult in charge felt there was nothing wrong with this.

I can recall times when I was in elementary school when our teacher left us alone for a few minutes, but I don't think that would ever be the case today. I went directly to my principal about this because the overall safety of the kids was in question. What if two of the kids got into a physical altercation while the teacher was out of the room and one of the children got hurt? A school district and school employee would probably be legally responsible for any damages if a student were injured when no one was supervising the child/class.

Another time I was out for about a week, and much to my amazement, the substitute disregarded my instructions after the first couple of days and then did what she wanted. I was shocked to think that any substitute teacher would deliberately ignore the lesson plan. I'm sure that some teachers tend to spend more time on the things that they are genuinely interested in or that they are more skilled in teaching. If a teacher enjoys teaching writing, then he/she is more likely to make time for this. On this particular occasion, my substitute had expertise in teaching art (something I lacked) and began doing art projects with my class for a good part of the day. I would never want to have a substitute again if that person disregarded my plans. In this case, I reported what had happened to my principal. The safety of the kids was not an issue here, but ignoring the wishes of the classroom teacher is not acceptable either. It was aggravating from my end too as an ill teacher who was spending two hours a day writing a lesson plan, only to have it ignored. Good substitutes develop a reputation among the staff too, and teachers request these people with much greater frequency. I never faced the challenge of subbing, but I think I would do my best to try to follow through on the teacher's lesson plan to the best of my ability, particularly since good substitutes moved to the top of the hiring list when teaching positions open.

The longer I taught, the more active a role I began to take in promoting those administrators who I felt were doing a good job. I felt my last principal, Tami Beall, was excellent, and I saw it as a moral responsibility to inform the superintendent and school board about the great job that I thought she was doing. As I approached retirement, even though I imagined that she would remain at our school longer than I, it was important to me that I felt the district was in good hands when I was leaving. I had so much of myself invested in my school, and I ultimately wanted Pine Hill to retain the excellent reputation that my colleagues and I had helped to create within the community.

One quality that I most admired about Tami was her extra effort to recognize anyone on the staff, regardless of their job. That kind of positive approach builds camaraderie and a sense of family among the employees. She also did random acts of kindness for everyone. I remember that my wife and I were taking a rare day off to travel to our son's last college football game in his senior year, and she took it upon herself to make up a basket of goodies for us, including snacks and a warm blanket. It was so thoughtful and the kind of gesture that speaks to the sort of person she is.

Tami also led by example. She spoke to the kids about making healthy decisions and getting regular exercise, but talking only gets you so far. Tami would be out there every Friday (weather permitting) to promote a healthy lifestyle by running laps with the kids at recess. She never bragged about her achievements, but she was quite the accomplished runner, competing in marathons and triathlons. She also formed a cross-country running team at Pine Hill for our K-3rd-grade students. I believe kids learn more when role models lead by example.

When working with a large group of teachers, you will find that some of your colleagues may feel differently than you about an administrator's job performance. It doesn't necessarily mean one colleague's assessment is right or wrong, but those different interactions can lead to different opinions.

If you have been a teacher for a long time, you are going to encounter administrators with different management styles. Some are very hands-off and seem to trust their staff to do the right thing, while others are so involved that they micromanage each decision made. It comes with the territory that principals/superintendents are going to have different styles, (like teachers) and you need to adjust and be flexible to handle those different approaches. I preferred administrators somewhere in the middle of these two styles. I liked it when my administrator had faith in us to do the right thing, but I also wanted to know I was working for a person who cared about what was happening in the school.

Administrators have a tough job, and they are not going to make everyone happy. The criticism that some of them receive is not always fair. However, there are times when you get less than what you should expect. There will be some situations in which you disagree with the administrator's decision, but when the administrator consults the staff, differing opinions are going to be easier to accept. Good administrators value the viewpoints of the people around them and work as part of a team. Fortunately, that was usually the case, but on rare occasions, we'd have someone with the attitude, "I'm the one in charge and if you don't like it, tough!"

Administrators are like anyone else in that they want to feel valued for the job they are doing. Given the criticism many administrators get, the occasional thank you or sincere compliment goes a long way. I would write my boss a thank you note when I felt like he/she was doing an awesome job. I only did this if my feelings were genuine. If I didn't think my administrator was doing a particularly good job, I would never comment on that to any board member or the parent community because I don't think that would be appropriate. If a parent complained about a principal to me (this did happen on occasion), I never expressed my opinion because I didn't think it was my place to be critiquing the performance of my boss or to undermine his/her credibility with the public.

One thing to be aware of is that administrators are often part of the ongoing collective bargaining negotiations that occur at a school between the district and the teachers' union. Depending on the district, the negotiating team usually included someone from the administration with their budgetary concerns. As a teacher who was part of the bargaining team for our teachers' union for a few years, I found that sometimes negotiations could be quite civil, but at other times they were confrontational. Both teachers and administrators should try to prevent this from becoming personal, but it is the administrator who sets the tone for these negotiations. The thing to keep in mind is that both sides still have to work with one another after the bargaining process. Maintaining a good working relationship throughout the process should be the ultimate goal.

One interesting thing I discovered about myself in negotiations was that I found it much easier to negotiate with someone I didn't already know on a personal basis. I have felt pretty comfortable when negotiating to buy a large item such as a house or a car with a relative stranger compared to bargaining a school contract with someone I worked with every day. The main reason for this was because the whole negotiation process feels different when you are negotiating with someone that you already have a good working relationship with, compared to someone who is not so close. The other difference for me was that I felt like I was operating on an equal playing field with someone I didn't know that well, but when it came to negotiating with someone whom I viewed as my boss, it didn't feel like we were coming from positions of equality. When it comes to negotiations at school, you are supposed to be equals, but it is hard to forget that the person you might be sitting across from in bargaining is normally your superior.

One of the curious things about the administrators with whom I worked involved observing the relationships that they developed with their staff. Some kept a very professional yet distant relationship, while others maintained an active social connection away from school. I think that this was up to the person and what they were comfortable with regarding the staff. Some administrators were likely to invite co-workers over to their home for social functions or to go out for drinks after work on the occasional Friday with everyone. I never thought less of an administrator who tried to remain a little more separated from his/her staff. Since we're all different, it comes down to that with which they are most comfortable.

I believe that my administrators appreciated when I was honest and straightforward with them. Try to maintain an open relationship. If, for example, you are interested in trying something new educationally in your classroom, I would keep the administrator apprised of this. If you have a suggestion for the whole staff, approach the administrator with your idea privately first. If you realize beforehand your administrator is supportive of a change that you are advocating for; you will not put him/her on the spot at a staff meeting without any advanced knowledge or discussion. There is a greater likelihood that your idea will be met with support If you discuss it ahead of time with your administrator.

Do not take a skillful administrator for granted. You may not realize how lucky you are to have an exceptional one until you have someone who isn't skilled at the job. An administrator who has the staff's support is much more likely to want to stay around than one who feels unappreciated. I worked for some fabulous administrators, but I also worked for some who were either just adequate or were not very good. The administrator at your school sets the tone for the school's environment and climate. I learned to keep my mouth shut and do my job if I worked for a poor one, but a subpar administrator can bring down the overall morale. I don't feel like it is healthy to complain day after day to your co-workers when you end up with a poor administrator because this further deteriorates a positive working environment.

Discipline

Every teacher has to deal with discipline. I could write a whole book on this topic alone as it is a vital element in any teacher's classroom. As I said in the introduction, being a good teacher is not that different from being a good parent. It is my opinion that love and discipline are the two main, critical ingredients in raising independent and happy children. The same is correct for the students in your class.

My own experiences with discipline have, quite naturally, shaped me into the type of person/teacher I am. I grew up in an era where most parents, including mine, spanked children when they misbehaved. My parents did a fantastic job raising my brothers and me, but that doesn't mean that I always agreed with everything they did. I know that after I spanked my son for the first time when he was little, I did not feel right about how that form of discipline felt for me. I decided from that day on that spankings would not be part of my approach to raising him. I know that some of my friends still use spankings as a method for disciplining their children. I'm not trying to tell them they are wrong for raising their kids in this manner, but I am saying that this approach didn't work for my wife or me. As our son grew up, we tended to send him to his room, and as he got older, we took away privileges from him when he misbehaved. Whatever method works for you as a parent, I think the most important thing is that you talk openly and honestly to your child after disciplining him/her. I viewed any disciplinary action as an opportunity to teach rather than to punish. We always ended up these discussions with a hug and a reminder to our son about how much we loved him.

My parents raised my brothers and me in a home that provided love and discipline. My mom and dad were indeed a united front, and despite all of the times I looked for a crack in their defense, I seldom found one. More than once when I was asking them if I could participate in some activity with my friends, I'd usually get a response like, "What did your mother say?" Not to outdone by Dad, my mom would usually say, "What did your father say?" They shared most of the same values and beliefs, so there was no opportunity to try and work over the weakest link.

My dad was the stronger disciplinarian of the two, and my mom tended to be the more nurturing parent. Mom was not a pushover when it came to discipline though. I was sadly mistaken if I thought I was going to put one over on her because she wasn't as intimidating as Dad, and she definitely could hold her own with us. My dad traveled quite a bit in his job. Mom was forced to handle the discipline while he was gone. I am the youngest of four boys, and we all turned out pretty well. We were generally well-behaved boys, but I'm sure there were times when we were a challenge to our parents.

I always loved my parents, but as I became an adult, I further appreciated the strong foundation they laid. Growing up in a good home with loving parents and three protective, older brothers, I didn't realize at the time how lucky I was to be born into such a stable family. I became more aware of things as I grew up and noticed that some of my friends came from families entirely different than ours. More than 50% of marriages end up in divorce, but the thought of my parents splitting up never entered my mind. Having that kind of stability is reassuring to a child. We weren't rich, but money never seemed to be an issue. We were the definition of a middle-class family, and I would describe my parents as being frugal and very responsible with their money. They were generous toward the causes that they believed in, and education was one of their priorities for us.

Many of my students were not as fortunate as I. Some of their families were having a rough time financially. Some children came to school without new clothes or new school supplies at the start of the year. Our school population had a relatively high rate of students who were receiving free or reduced lunches based on their family income. Some children didn't have jackets or sweatshirts on cold and windy days. I always had a few students who came to school with poor hygiene. That not only provided challenges for them but for the students who sat near them. As children grow older and their bodies begin to change, this becomes more of an issue. I sometimes had children who complained that their academic partner smelled. Some of the older 5th and 6th-grade students who I taught were also not as understanding or as sensitive as I would have liked them to be in these circumstances. We were fortunate to have a program at our school called Healthy Start. This program supported families who needed clothing, food, backpacks, and products like shampoo, soap, and deodorant to improve their hygiene.

Some of my students did not have stable home environments. A few of their parents had a hard time managing their own lives, let alone being a role model for their children. Some families were dealing with physical abuse, drug or alcohol issues, mental health problems, and many other factors that made it difficult for them to be the stabilizing force that their children needed. At times, I would have a few children who had a parent in jail or prison. There were also parents who lacked the educational ability to help their children even when they wanted to. Parents could even be hostile toward the school or teacher because of attitudes that they formed years ago when they went through the school system.

Why does it matter what kind of home your students come from when it comes to discipline? It matters because some parents use discipline to punish their child rather than to teach them right from wrong. If, for example, a child is using cuss words or inappropriate language and the parent becomes angry and disciplines the child by forcing a bar of soap into the child's mouth, is this type of discipline teaching the child anything? If anything, it is probably doing more harm than good. If a parent or teacher explodes in a fit of rage, we are teaching children that this is the appropriate way to respond when someone does something we don't like.

Discipline is critical when raising children. To ignore antisocial behavior, in effect, is teaching children that there are no consequences for their actions. The key to discipline is that it should provide the child a lesson in a firm but caring way. If I learned that one of my students was being disrespectful to one of the supervisors at school, I'm sure I would be a little upset with the student. If I merely impose some punishment without talking to the child, then the discipline loses its impact and isn't likely to change any behavior in the child. Imagine that the consequence was to have the student miss the next two recesses. I would argue that this is likely to have little to no effect. What if the punishment imposed involved humiliating the student in some fashion? Let's say the teacher/supervisor lost their cool and yelled at the child, "Since you are going to act like a spoiled brat, then I am going to treat you like the baby you are! I want you to suck on this pacifier all recess until you have learned your lesson!" This form of discipline isn't going to make someone behave better. In fact, it is quite likely that the situation will escalate when the child refuses to follow the teacher's/supervisor's unreasonable directions and challenges their authority.

What ultimately happens is that the adult has made the situation worse. Even if the child complies to some unreasonable discipline are they going to feel remorse for what they have done? On the other hand, if a teacher first gives the child a chance to settle down with a brief time-out, talks to the child calmly but firmly, gets the student to think about the power of hurtful words, and then suggests a more appropriate type of discipline, the student may actually learn something from the experience.

What is an appropriate type of discipline in this situation? I would suggest having the student write a sincere letter of apology to the supervisor. If the student needed help in doing this, then I would guide him. I would recommend the student wait until the end of recess and present the letter of apology to the supervisor. It is imperative that the child faces the person that they have wronged and try to apologize. I might even suggest that the student could help the supervisor in some manner for the next recess to fully make the point that there are consequences for our actions. Maybe the "help" is something like looking for kids on the playground that are using appropriate play-ground behavior. Perhaps the student could pick up trash or sweep a sidewalk for the supervisor. The point is that it is always better to discipline a student by having the child do something positive for the school, rather than writing fifty sentences or sitting in the office for the next two recesses. So, this child has completed the appropriate discipline by writing a sincere letter of apology. He listened to how that person felt when he/she was talked to disrespectfully. He has done something productive for the school, and, thus, has maintained his dignity while hopefully learning something in the process.

What about a different type of scenario? Let's say a middle school youth vandalized someone's personal property away from school. Getting angry, yelling, or grounding that child for a week is not go-ing to have the effect that a more meaningful and productive form of discipline might have. In a situation like this, it would be more use-ful to have the child think about the money it will cost to repair this item. If I were the child's parent, I would first talk to him about how he would feel if another person ruined one of his prized possessions. I would then look for ways that the child could do some physical work to earn money to pay for the damaged property. Perhaps washing the car, mowing the lawn, or trimming the bushes might earn the funds toward repaying the damage. When the child has completed the nec-essary jobs, it is vital for him to face the victim, apologize, and hand over the necessary cash for the damage. That brings closure in an impactful way. Handling the discipline in this manner is much more likely to make a lasting impression rather than merely grounding the child. It is always better to do something positive to try and make a situation right.

New teachers should find out if the school even has a disci-pline plan. If so, is it something that everyone follows? A schoolwide discipline plan becomes pointless if a majority of staff members don't follow the guidelines or ignore them altogether. The success or failure of a discipline plan is that it must empower all those who supervise the children in your school. Bus drivers, cafeteria workers, playground supervisors, and even custodians should be familiar with the disciplinary plan and be trusted and supported when following it. If the support staff doesn't have that authority, children will learn that they only have to follow the rules if the principal or teacher is around.

Our school developed a cohesive discipline plan to be followed throughout the school. There were three fundamental rules: (1) Be Safe (2) Be Respectful (3) Be Responsible. When any adult in the school saw a student following the rules, the adult could quickly write down the student's name on a Panda Paw to give to that student. Each adult in the school had a stack of these small notes that could be given out. Children redeemed their Panda Paws (our school mascot was the panda) for things in the child's classroom. One of our teachers introduced the concept of "brag tags" to the rest of us. Every student had a necklace hanging somewhere in the class. These necklaces held the brag tags. A brag tag was a small token that fit onto the chain. When students attended school assemblies, they would often wear their necklaces. Students earned brag tags for many things (perfect attendance, being on time, academic accomplishments, exemplary behavior, etc.) At the end of each school year, the students got to take their brag tags home.

I liked handling most discipline myself, but there will undoubtedly be times when you, as a teacher, need to let the vice-principal or principal deal with particularly challenging situations. Sometimes there were kids from several classes involved in a dispute, and it was impractical for me to go around and try to gather all of the involved children to get to the bottom of it.

Your principal or vice-principal is a critical figure in disciplinary matters. It is crucial that this is someone you can trust and has your back. A weak administrator who avoids dealing with discipline or caves into intimidating parents can be incredibly frustrating.

Over the course of your career, you will probably work with administrators who are both strong and weak concerning the handling of disciplinary matters. I had principals tell me, "Why don't you just handle this?" when it seemed to be a case in which someone above me should be addressing the problem. If I had an administrator like this, then I knew that I was going to have to be able to take on more of these situations myself. Part of the frustrating part of this was spending more time on discipline meant that I would have less time to spend on teaching and preparing for future lessons.

Give considerable thought and planning about discipline weeks before a school year has begun. On the first day of school, send parents your homework policy and discipline plan. If your school has an effective discipline plan in place, this should be the guide. Develop positive relationships and open lines of communication with parents immediately at the start of each school year. If parents never hear from you until there is a problem, then they are less likely to trust and support you. On the other hand, if you have already developed a positive rapport with a parent/guardian, you are much more likely to receive the support you need from them when necessary.

As I mentioned before, one of the things I did each year was to meet with my students' teachers from the previous year to see if they could offer me any insight about individual kids. While I took in all of this information about students and generally found it to be helpful, I also knew that I had to have an open mind when it came to my students. If I started my year off with the thought that a specific child was going to be horrible in my class based solely on the experiences of others, then this would be unfair to the child. You have to keep an open mind and set high standards for your students. Children will generally rise to higher but reasonable expectations.

Kids often act out when there is something troublesome or hurtful going on in their lives that makes them angry. Maybe one of your students was a discipline problem the previous year because he/she was going through a difficult or challenging time. Did the child's parents just split up? Was there a death in the family that upset their usual way of life? I have witnessed some incredible turnarounds in behavior over the years. I remember one year when I had an incredibly sweet boy in my class who was low academically. While he struggled to do well in school, I always thought of "Kenny" as a big, lovable teddy bear. He got along with everybody, and his classmates liked him a lot.

I was taking part in a teacher's workshop and by coincidence ran into his teacher from the previous year. She had heard that Kenny was attending our school now, and asked how he was doing. Much to my complete shock and amazement, she painted an entirely different picture of the student I knew. She said that he had been an enormous discipline problem with an explosive temper. That was so far afield from the experience I had with Kenny that I thought we must have been talking about different children. At his first parent conference that year, I learned from Kenny's grandfather that Kenny had been through a horrible situation the previous year. He had been separated from his biological brother, removed from his dad's house, and had begun living with his grandpa. Kenny's grandpa said that in spite of the horrible conditions that Kenny had been living in, he missed his brother and was longing for the time when they could be reunited. It was a truly heartbreaking story, but it might explain why the previous year's teacher saw a much different student than I did. That was a re-minder to me that you can't always make assumptions about children based solely on what the previous teacher tells you.

My first year of teaching I was supposed to be getting a chal-lenging child from our sister school whom I will call "Kayla." I heard many stories of how she was the terror of the school, and all of the tales I heard regarding the previous teacher's interactions with her seemed awful! I heard that the teacher had gotten so angry with her that he was chasing her around campus one day. I learned that she had called her teacher every word in the book, and she was prone to having some pretty dramatic behavior issues. I think that she had deservedly earned her reputation, but my interactions with her were much different. She certainly wasn't an easy student to deal with, but she wasn't anything like the child she had been portrayed to be. I don't want this to come across like I just had a magic touch with this particular student or that the cause of her problems was the previous teacher because neither of those statements would be accurate. I'm only mentioning this because not everything you hear about a student will always be the same for you. When she was mouthy with me or refused to do what she was initially instructed to do, I didn't stop everything and get into a power struggle with her. I would tell her in a quiet, earnest manner what I expected her to do, and then I resumed whatever I was doing. When she didn't get the reaction she expected from me, she would eventually get around to following my directions. It just took her longer than the average student to do it. I think if I had challenged her by raising my voice or by trying to intimidate her, she would have responded by acting out more. As a first-year teacher of 5th and 6th graders, I learned that year it was often better to give a student a little more space and time to do the right thing rather than to challenge him/her in front of their peers.

I later tried to praise her privately when she made good choices. There were times she was a handful! When I needed to, I disciplined her or sent her to the principal, but this happened less and less as the year progressed. As with any disciplinary action I took, the most critical part was the talking (and hopefully learning) that followed. I reminded myself throughout the year to try to have these discussions after things had calmed down rather than in the heat of the moment.

If there is one piece of advice that I would give to all beginning teachers, it would be to communicate, communicate, and then communicate some more with your students and their families in regard to discipline. Of course, there are many different ways to go about reaching out to parents. Face-to-face communication was probably the best method. Many times, the more practical way for me was to speak to a parent over the phone, but this can be hard to do, especially if the parent is at work.

In the past few years, some of the teachers at my site were using an app called Class Dojo. This program enables parents to receive behavior updates over their smartphones during a regular school day to determine how their child is doing. The advantages of a program like this are that the feedback provided by the teacher is often received instantaneously. You can also take photos and share videos of what is going on in your classroom. Parents could then pick up their child after school and even have a brief conversation with the teacher about what happened that day. I know that this didn't work well for me because many days it seemed like I hit the ground running and never had time during a typical day to even sit and think about doing something like this. I did my parental communication after school when I could think and articulate precisely what I wanted to say to a parent about his/her child. However, I know that several of my colleagues just loved this program, and finding the time to utilize it must not have been an issue for them. One of my preferred methods of communication was sending the parents a weekly note.

In the course of an average school year, there are lots of incidents that need to be dealt with immediately. When this happened, I either called the parents after school or in the evening at home. When something of a severe nature occurs, you can't wait a week to report it to a parent.

As I previously mentioned, I used paychecks and bank books with my sixth graders to support my discipline plan. When I moved down to teach 2nd and 3rd grades, I got rid of the banking system because that was beyond the capability of most of my students, but I still had a system in place that supported the school's discipline policy. The kids would earn "bonus points" throughout the week for completing their homework, having good behavior, returning parent notes with a parental signature, and for doing extra credit. I liked this system mostly because it was not biased toward the smartest kids in the class. Children who worked hard and had good habits were on an equal playing field with the brightest kids in the class.

At the end of the week, I would post a top ten for all of the highest point earners in the class. Since class sizes in California for primary grades are generally smaller than for upper grades, the top ten might be about half of the students in my class. The kids who made it onto the top ten knew that they would be getting a prize of some kind when I held a raffle. Raffles were held every five weeks in my class, and the kids learned a lot from this experience. The kids found out about probability and chance. I designed the raffle so that the children who were on the top ten more often than their classmates would get the first pick of the prizes. Each child could only win once during the drawing, but the kids who were in more often got to pick before the others who weren't in as many times. We would keep going until every student who was in the raffle won something, and some students had to sit there watching their classmates win while they didn't get anything. This might seem like a cruel thing to do, but I was merely trying to teach them the importance of working hard and completing their homework. I would often try to tell my students that in the real world they had to be willing to compete with others. Someone else was going to get their job, or they would likely be passed over for a promotion if they weren't willing to put in the time necessary. Many times, children who did not win a prize were motivated and improved their work habits in the next cycle before the next raffle. I felt that it was important for them to learn that they could control their destiny if they were willing to work hard.

While I'm on the discussion of using prizes to reward kids for hard work and good behavior, I know that I'm opening up a debate on another topic. Should we even offer rewards in school in the first place? I have had this discussion many times over the years with several of my colleagues. People I respect come down on both sides of this issue. Most of the research indicates that rewards don't really change behavior over the long run. I also know that some of my colleagues found it offensive to give out prizes. Some hold the belief that intrinsic rewards are enough for children, and we are doing them a disservice by providing tangible objects. The problem with this approach is that it assumes all kids are going to be motivated intrinsically. While this might be nice in theory, I think the reality is that not all people feel this way. When I was a kid in elementary school, I often behaved a certain way because I didn't want to get into trouble. As I matured and started to think more about my place in the world, my motivation for doing the right things wasn't so narrow or self-centered. I became motivated for broader, and perhaps, nobler reasons. I began to think about doing something because it was the right thing to do rather than doing it to avoid getting into trouble. I started paying attention to trying to make my community better, not just for me, but for generations of people to come.

I feel like it is appropriate to occasionally sprinkle in some tangible reward for children who are doing their job. While I don't think we should continuously reward kids with an overabundance of things for doing their job as students, I definitely feel like there is nothing wrong with offering occasional incentives. Competing in today's modern world is a part of life. Teaching students that hard work can pay off is an essential lesson for everyone to learn. As much as I enjoyed being a teacher, part of what motivated me to get to work was to take care of my family. My wife and I wanted our son to get a good education, and it was important to us that we gave him this opportunity. We are an average, middle-class family and having a nice home and being able to send our son to a good college were things that got me going as I pushed myself to go to work each Saturday morning.

When athletes train and have the self-discipline and self-motivation to go work out or pay attention to their diet, aren't they essentially trying to make sacrifices to reach their goals? This is not that different from providing the occasional tangible incentive to students. You do not need to go out and spend a lot of money on incentives. I often found lots of things at dollar stores that the kids liked. I also worked with local businesses for donations and had parents who wanted to contribute something to my class raffles.

Memorable Students

The greatest gift that teaching consistently gives is the building of relationships. You develop relationships with your colleagues, your students' families, and of course, the students themselves. I treasured all of these connections, but the most important to me was with my students. That was a relationship that lasted for more than just the year that I taught a student in my class.

Teaching is different than most other professions in that you don't always see the results of your efforts until years have passed. In so many other industries, the fruits of your labor are quite apparent because they're right in front of you. For example, if your job is that of a construction worker, you can see the progress that you are making on the job as you go along. Artists can see the growth they're making every hour put into a project. Teachers, on the other hand, get some feedback during the year when they observe how a student has mastered a skill, but the real payoff comes later.

I started a tradition of giving students my address at the end of the school year in hopes that I might hear from some of them during the summer. I always heard from some, and a few kids even continued to stay in touch as the years passed. It was exciting to get a letter from a former student and hear about what he/she was doing now. I continue to stay in touch with many of my former students via letter writing or Facebook. It is very special to me that I have managed to keep in contact with some of my former students as they become adults, get married, and have children of their own.

I always looked forward to visits from former students. Many years I had visits from former students who dropped in to let me know they were graduating from junior high or high school and ready to start the next chapter in their lives. The fact that they returned years later was a reminder to me of the impact we make in our students' lives. I felt proud that I had a part in helping to mold my students into responsible, young adults. When word got out in my final year of teaching that I was going to be retiring, I was incredibly touched when some of my former students dropped in periodically to wish me well in retirement. The fact that they cared enough to stop by their former elementary school to visit their old teacher was a gift I will never forget.

The manner in which people communicate with one another today is one of those interesting case studies in human behavior. I am a people watcher, and I find it fascinating to watch how people interact with one another. I think it is somewhat amusing to see a family eating out together and to observe them looking at their phones and texting their friends instead of interacting with the people who are actually in front of them. Perhaps because I was born in a different era, I was slow to embrace the technological changes in our modern world. However, many of my friends who are my age jumped right in and saw its many advantages. When I was a kid, people were still communicating by snail mail instead of via computers and cell phones. One of my annual projects was to have my students write a letter to a family member or friend.

Quite a few of my students didn't even know how to address an envelope, and many had never received a letter in the mail before. I am hardly that guy advocating for "the good old days." It is crazy not to take advantage of technology, and if I were a new teacher, I would fully embrace it.

Many of my friends became involved with Facebook long before I decided to take the plunge. I see both positives and negatives with social media. I have seen plenty of examples of cyberbullying and other negative behaviors, but when I joined a few years ago, I had no idea that I would get in touch with so many previous students of mine who are now adults. Many of them reached out to me via this form of communication. I was curious as to what happened to some of my prior students, and Facebook has allowed me to uncover some of those mysteries. Several former students wanted me to know that I was an important role model or teacher in their development. There is great satisfaction in knowing that I contributed to students realizing their potential. It reinforces the feeling I've always held within me that good teachers and role models matter. Some of my former students' parents have contacted me and thanked me for being a good teacher and role model in helping to shape their child's development. Plenty of jobs pay more than teaching, but I think I would be hard-pressed to find another profession that would ultimately pay me back so many years down the road.

I never really thought that much about how many children I interacted with as a teacher, but the number has to be well over 1,000. Since I live in the same city where I taught my entire career, I continue to run into former students and their families practically every week when I am out and about. The bond between a teacher and student lasts for a lifetime. Running into a former student (many of whom are now adults) always brings a smile to my face. I get great satisfaction coming across a former student who has become a responsible teenager or young adult. On most occasions, these outcomes were generally predictable, but at other times I was shocked or at least mildly surprised by what became of a former student. Children normally grew up happy and responsible if they came from a loving, stable home in which education was a top priority. Unfortunately, there also were students raised in dysfunctional situations with poor role models who sadly grew up to repeat the cycle. It was discouraging to think that many of these children would grow up and lead the same kind of lives that their parents or negative role models had.

One of the things that I wrestled with the most as a young teacher was the idea that I couldn't rescue them all. I spent many restless nights trying to think about how to reach a child who had so many negative obstacles to overcome. At the same time, this doesn't mean that we should accept the outcome without trying to help our students. I would be interested in understanding how and why some children amazingly overcome such odds to grow into productive members of society.

There are individual children that you immediately connect with as a teacher. You know it right away just in the way that they react toward you. You will teach children who are cooperative, respectful, and self-disciplined. They are the kind of students any teacher would love to have in class, and they get along with just about everyone. Some children do well with just about anyone as their teacher, but some kids do better with one type of teacher over another. There are a lot of different reasons for this. It isn't always because one teacher is better than another, and I suppose it is not that different from why one person prefers rock and roll to country music or why some people like eggs for breakfast rather than cereal. It merely has to do with personal preference. Since we all have our likes and dislikes, it isn't surprising that some children seem to do better with one teacher than another. I have been on both sides of the coin before. You may have a difficult child who another teacher will talk about in glowing terms. It is only natural to think, "Am I doing something wrong?" On the other hand, I had several students who seemed to thrive in my class when they didn't do well with other teachers.

Occasionally, a child whom I didn't feel very strongly connected to would come back to visit a few years later and catch me off guard by telling me what an excellent role model I was. Although I may not have verbalized it, inside my reaction was something like, "I was???" The point that I'm making is that we should never underestimate the influence that we, as teachers, can have on children. While lots of teachers inspire their students in positive and admirable ways, there are sad instances where teachers affect a student negatively.

I put a lot of responsibility on myself to be a role model to my students. I remember when former basketball great and current commentator, Charles Barkley, once said, "I don't believe professional athletes should be role models. I believe that parents should be role models." I think that what Mr. Barkley was saying was that athletes should not be role models for kids just because they happen to be good at some particular athletic skill. While I agree with this sentiment, I also know that sometimes some of our students did not have good role models to emulate in their families. I taught many kids who needed a positive male influence in their lives. I felt that a significant part of my job as a teacher went far beyond what a child learned in the core academic material or the grade level standards. The most important lessons I wanted my students to learn were often not found in textbooks—things like hard work, achieving your dreams, respecting others' differences, learning to work with a partner or team, and learning from your mistakes. These were all qualities I hoped that I could pass on to my students. The times when I was the hardest on myself were the moments I felt that I had let my students down in one of those areas. I welcomed and appreciated the opportunity to be a role model for my students. Most of the time I think I did an excellent job of that, but part of being a human being is realizing that we aren't perfect. If I believed I had messed up in some way toward my class or an individual, I knew the correct thing to do was to offer a sincere apology to that person or group. Kids are learning from us all the time, and how we react when we make a mistake teaches them to admit fault and accept responsibility for their actions.

Teachers should embrace this immense responsibility. I considered it a blessing, and not a curse, to have been given this opportunity to inspire my students. Sure, plenty of professions pay more. Yes, some jobs don't have so much constant change and instability, but how many people go to work day after day and say that they were given this fantastic opportunity to be a role model and honestly make a difference in their community? Getting hugs every day from your students doesn't hurt either.

My wife was a dedicated preschool teacher and director for her entire working career. She taught a wide array of kids too. Many of her kids and families were terrific, but there were children that she first encountered at three to four years of age with difficult obstacles to overcome. Sadly, they had already been given two strikes because of their home situation. The chances that they would somehow overcome these beginnings when they were born into poverty, crime, violence or a life with unstable parents were slim at best. These were adults who couldn't even seem to manage their own lives. The reality is that many of these children have their lives mapped out (good or bad) even by the time they are in preschool. The most rewarding aspect of my career were the times when I witnessed some of these children overcome their difficult situations and break the cycle of dysfunction.

One of the things that most people don't realize (I sure didn't) is that many of our students serve as teachers to us as well. The things that I learned from my students are virtues that I tried to live by in my own life. The qualities that I admired in my students such as perseverance, kindness, generosity, curiosity, optimism, and too many others to mention inspired me to want to be a better teacher and person.

I've often maintained that adults can learn a lot just by watching kids and that the teacher/student relationship is mutually beneficial. There are some things that kids are better at than adults. I don't just mean things like playing video games. I'm referring to those human qualities that help a person in life.

One beautiful characteristic that many of my younger students possessed was the ability to forgive one another. It is human nature to get your feelings hurt by the actions of others. Human beings can be sensitive. It is normal to be upset when someone you love or respect says something negative to you or about you. I was often impressed that a lot of younger children could get past these things better than many adults I know. The idea that one child would go weeks, months or even years without talking to one another because of some specific incident is not something I ever witnessed once with younger children. Adults can be so stubborn at times and let their situations fester for years because their pride gets in the way instead of just apologizing, making up, and starting over.

Children moved and inspired me with their general kindness and thoughtfulness. In fact, I spend a lot of time defending kids when my generation starts complaining about "kids these days," as if there was only an overabundance of good kids when we were children. I think this is a fallacy, and I see plenty of outstanding, young people who give me great hope for the future.

Even though the children I was touched and inspired by are real, I think it best to keep their names private, so I am using fictitious names. One young girl, "Janet," came from a difficult situation. When she was in my class, her father was out of the picture. The biggest positive that she had in her life was a strong mom and family. She had quite a few older siblings, and they were a very close, well-knit family. She was an excellent student, and she was a wonderful friend to many of the other kids in the class. She was a little on the quiet side when she was in my class, but I never worried about her because she seemed to have a strong sense of right and wrong.

One day she told me privately that she had been saving up her money so that she could take her family on a summer vacation. She was an honest kid, and I assumed this was probably her true intention, but I was skeptical that a 2nd grader could earn enough money to be able to take her family anywhere. Of course, I didn't want to burst her bubble by telling her that this could never happen, so I asked her a few more questions to see what her plan was. She told me that she had been working all year (we were probably halfway through the school year at this point) doing chores around the house in order to help pay for her family's trip. She wanted to take her family on a vacation and pay for the motel that they would be staying at. She told me how much money she had earned, and how much more money she needed to pay for the motel and to be able to take her family out to dinner. Since her figures were in the ballpark of what the costs would really be, I began to think her story was legitimate. It was just amazing to comprehend that a child this age would have developed such a goal and was actually well on the way to making it happen. At first, I wanted to give her the remaining balance because I was so moved by her determination, heart, and thoughtfulness. Upon reflecting about the situation a little more, I realized that this was one of those moments in her life that she was going to remember forever. I told my wife that I wanted to help her family financially to ensure they could take their trip, but I would wait to see if Janet was able to raise the remaining funds. For the rest of the year, I would check in with her occasionally to see if she was still working toward her goal. She told me that she was and always seemed to know how much more money she needed to raise. I have tears in my eyes years later as I am writing this because it was one of the most inspiring things I had ever witnessed. To think it was achieved by a seven-year-old made it all the more moving.

When I heard from Janet years later, I discovered that her family did take that trip after all, and that made me feel happy. She wanted me to know that her mom had paid for their vacation, and she was able to use the money she had saved for her own needs. What I do believe though with certainty is that Janet learned a lot from this experience in her life. I'm sure she learned that hard work does help you reach your goals and that she could accomplish a tough challenge if she were determined.

One of the best parts of this whole story came years later when I ran into Janet working at a fast food restaurant in her senior year of high school. We hugged, and I told her it was great to see her. When I asked what was going on in her life and how long she had been working there, I learned that she began her job with the intention of buying a car for herself and had recently accomplished that goal. I didn't say anything to her about how I remembered her reaching a hard goal when she was in my class in 2nd grade, but all I could think of on my ride home was how a strong-minded little girl had grown up and was now a determined and responsible young adult. Today, Janet is in college and studying to become a medical assistant. That doesn't surprise me in the least because she was the kind of person who was always looking out for others.

How are 2nd or 3rd graders supposed to make sense of things when a parent is out of their lives for whatever reason? Many of their classmates came from stable families with two parents. You have to think about these things ahead of time if you are making a Father's Day or Mother's Day project in class and a child has little or virtually no relationship with a parent. When a child said something like, "I never met my dad," or, "My mom is in prison," I would see if they could think of another adult role model (aunt, uncle, older cousin, trusted family friend, or even former teacher) who they thought they might like to make a gift for. If the child seemed genuinely distressed about the whole situation, I might ask my student if he/she wanted to do a different activity to help out the class (e.g., sharpen pencils, sort papers, or go help out in another classroom).

Another student who I had the pleasure of teaching was "Laura." She was the kind of student who had an awful lot of difficult circumstances in her life to overcome. When Laura came to my class, I learned that she was living with her aunt and uncle. Part of her story involved the fact that she had no relationship with her mom because her mother had turned to a life of drug abuse. She did have a relationship with her father, but this was more challenging because he was in prison during the year that I taught Laura. In fact, a good part of that year, Laura was excited because her dad was scheduled to be soon released. I developed a close teacher/student relationship with Laura, and she would bring in the letters she received from her dad and let me read them. Having neither of her parents full time in her life, Laura had difficult obstacles to overcome.

Fortunately, her aunt and uncle had assumed custody of her and provided a stable and loving home. I saw them as heroes in her life because they were the lifeline and stability that Laura needed. During the school year I got to know her aunt and uncle pretty well, and I could see that they were doing their best to help raise Laura. When Laura's dad was scheduled to be released, I remember that she was extra excited the week before. She kept coming in to school each day with a countdown of days until she would be reunited with her dad. Finally, the day arrived when her family was going to drive down and pick him up. I can imagine the disappointment she must have felt when they found out upon arrival that his release was going to be delayed because of an altercation he'd had with another inmate.

When Laura returned to school a few days later, quite naturally my first question to her was how the reunion with her dad went. She bravely seemed to accept the delay in stride even though I knew she must have been heartbroken. She was happy she had a chance to visit her dad in prison. A couple of days later I spoke to Laura's aunt and asked her what happened and how Laura was dealing with the disappointment. Her aunt told me with tears in her eyes that they drove all the way there not having a clue that the dad was not going to be released. She said that Laura had handled it so bravely (better than her), and I was so moved when she told me that Laura had been looking forward to having me meet her dad. After hearing that, there was no way I was going to let my student down. I told her aunt to please let me know in the summer when Laura's dad got out because I wanted to take Laura and her dad out to lunch and meet him. I stayed in touch with them and at the start of the new school year, I followed through with my promise. It was a little awkward at first, but by the time we left I was very glad that I had a chance to meet him. He had paid his debt to society, and the day after our lunch he was going to be starting a new job as a mechanic. For the sake of Laura and her family, I hope that she re-establishes a great relationship with her father and that he can be the kind of role model that she deserves.

"Emily" was a 5th grader with whom I shared a special connection. I don't recall the exact situation, but she did not have a dad in her life. I feel for single parents because they have an enormous job of trying to raise a child and still have time to work, shop, cook, pay the bills, drive the kid(s) to their extracurricular events and all of the other things that are hard for two-parent families. Emily was a quiet kid, but I was optimistic about her future if given a fair opportunity. I do believe she was one of those kids who just seemed to need a positive male role model in her life. One day the kids and I were writing in our journals about the people in our lives who were most important to us. Of course, a lot of kids wrote about parents, siblings, other relatives, and classmates. Emily wrote a very touching piece about how I was one of the most important people in her life. She wrote that I was like a dad to her and that sometimes she wished that I was her dad. It was sweet and heartfelt. I think she moved out of the area the next year and I never knew what became of her, but this was, once again, an example to me of how important teachers are.

Many of my fondest memories of teaching centered around watching students blossom and become leaders. One fun activity I did in 6th grade a few times in my career was to have an election in our class. The candidates vied for the position of "Teacher for a Day." I discussed my idea with my administrator ahead of time and learned that she was completely supportive of my plan. Any student who wanted to run for this position, first had to give a speech describing what he/she would do if elected "teacher". Kids listed their qualifications and told their classmates about their plans for the day. Many of the kids gave thoughtful speeches, and some gave considerable thought to their lesson plan. Following the speeches, we held a secret ballot, and the kids voted for their "Teacher for a Day."

One year a student who I'll refer to as "Gloria" was selected by her classmates to serve as teacher. She had a fantastic idea to center her day around Mexico/Spain, even though she wasn't a Hispanic child. If I recall, I believe she had been taking Spanish lessons somewhere, which is where I think her idea originated. She planned a whole day (with only a little help from me) of teaching the kids numbers, colors, and vocabulary in Spanish. She gave a cooking demonstration and made the kids some traditional foods to try. Gloria also taught the class some songs in Spanish. At one point in the day, the kids painted the Mexican flag. For P.E., she even had a piñata that the kids got to break open. It was a fantastic all-around day!

The reason it was particularly memorable for me was that Gloria was not one of those kids who had a natural stage personality. In fact, she was quite shy at the start of the year and rarely raised her hand to take part in the class. The fact that Gloria could develop this much confidence by the end of the year warmed my heart and made me proud. I lost track of her over the years, but I wondered if she ever considered becoming a teacher after this positive experience.

Our district hired four new teachers as replacements for those of us who retired the year I left. I'm sure it was just an odd coincidence, but that year was the first time that no males were teaching at my school. I think this was unfortunate because I always felt it was important, especially for elementary children, to have positive male and female role models in their lives. I know that I worked with many outstanding male and female colleagues, and I witnessed plenty of times when a child needed the touch of a female or male teacher depending on the circumstances in life. In fact, I think the school was operating best when there was a broad cross-section of teachers with different backgrounds. I always thought it was essential to have teachers of many different age groups as well. It certainly was beneficial to have experienced teachers on staff, but having a balance of young, enthusiastic educators was a good thing too.

While I cared about all of my students, it was important to remember my role as a teacher. You don't want to cross into anything resembling an inappropriate relationship. I've always been an affectionate person, and I frequently like to hug friends when I see them. On the other hand, I never wanted to give one of my students (or anyone else for that matter) the wrong impression. I often worked with students individually or in small groups after school because I wanted to help them, but when I did, I tried to leave my door open at all times. When I taught older, upper elementary children, I kept a little more distance from them. I do know that I read about teachers who ran into trouble because they crossed a line concerning a healthy teacher/student relationship.

While I tried to attend at least one extracurricular event of any student who invited me during a typical school year, I always talked to the parent(s) ahead of time to let them know I was planning on attending. One year a student in my class invited me to his birthday party, and I decided to make an appearance. What transpired next, though, was that other kids in the class asked me to subsequent birthday parties. As time passed, I became aware that I had created this problem for myself. I realized that it was just a matter of time before I got tired of going to birthday parties or a child would get his/her feelings hurt if I wasn't able to attend. I decided to pull the plug on this.

I taught with another teacher friend of mine who gave his students a gift certificate to a local ice cream shop on their birthday, and he even took some kids for the day to go to a baseball game to San Francisco. Some kids liked to bring in a treat for the whole class on their birthday, but even simple gestures like this can present unintended consequences. Some religions do not honor birthdays, and it could be awkward for those kids who weren't allowed to celebrate, especially when some of their peers, who didn't understand, might ask them why they couldn't have a treat.

Another thing that can be hard around holidays is that not everyone celebrates in the same way. I had students who might not recognize Christmas in their family, and you need to provide an alternative assignment (often in another classroom) if a student can't take part in making a Christmas ornament or work on a Halloween art project.

On a somber note, I don't know if you are ever prepared to deal with a death of a student or student's family member. Fortunately, this happened only a handful of times. Each time was hard and presented its own set of challenges. The first time it happened was when I was teaching a 5th grade class. That was one of the best groups of kids I ever had during my career—filled with a lot of delightful kids. Probably, the most challenging boy in the class was "Fred." He wasn't a naughty kid, but he was testing from the minute he arrived until the minute he left school. He reminded me of one of those wind-up toys that move around frenetically and never stops. He was the kind of kid who today would probably be put on some drug to help him focus. Very few children received any medication to help them concentrate when I first started teaching. I think that today far more kids are medicated than probably should be, but ADD and ADHD have become a popular diagnosis in the 21st century.

It was hard to get upset with Fred because he never really did anything mean, but he did manage to get on a lot of kids' nerves because he made it difficult to work around him. I had a soft spot for Fred because I could see he had a good heart, even though he regularly tested everyone's patience. I lived within five to ten minutes driving distance from my school. It was just about the right distance away from school for me because I was close without living right next to a bunch of kids from my class. (It's nice to have a little separation from home and work to maintain some privacy.) Fred, however, lived in my neighborhood, and occasionally he would come over to visit. On this particular Sunday afternoon, he showed up on my doorstep to tell me he would not be at school the following day. When I asked him why, he gave me the most heartbreaking news, "My brother was killed last night in a car accident."

I had already heard something about the incident on television earlier that day, but at that point, the identity of the victim was still unreleased. There is nothing that can prepare you for how to deal with such a devastating event. I don't even remember what I said to him, but I'm sure there wasn't anything that I was going to be able to tell him at that moment to make it better. That was only my 2nd year of teaching, and at that point in my life, I had had very few experiences with death. What could I possibly do to help ease the tremendous shock and pain that he must have been going through at the time? As I recall, he did not return to school for another week. When he did return, we, fortunately, had the services of a school psychologist and school counselor who spent a good part of the rest of the year regularly meeting with Fred to try and help him through this tragedy, and he received counseling services away from school as well.

One of the most tragic situations I can recall happened a few years later. One of the most delightful families I ever had the pleasure of teaching was made up of a father, mother, and their two daughters. The girls were two years apart in age. When you are a teacher for several years, one of the cool things about education is, inevitably, you will teach the siblings of some of your former students. Sometimes we get to know the parents of our students pretty well, especially when you have already taught an older sibling before. You will teach a lot of awesome kids in your career, but these two sisters ("Shannon" and "Sharon") were right near the top of my list. They were smart, kind, athletic, and very sweet kids who never gave me a moment of difficulty. Sharon was the younger of the two girls, and both of the kids participated in youth soccer growing up. The year after Sharon was in my class was the only time I have ever had one of my student's parents pass away (up to that point).

To make matters worse, the girls' dad died quite unexpectedly. The circumstances surrounding his death couldn't have been more devastating to the family. The soccer season had just finished for the year, and the kids and their families were having a gathering at our school on the weekend. In the middle of a soccer game between the parents and the kids, Shannon's and Sharon's dad collapsed and was taken by ambulance to the hospital. Tragically, he had sustained a heart attack and died right on the big field on our playground where the kids played every recess. To make this sad event even more horrific for those involved, several other kids (some who I taught) and their families witnessed this event.

Since many years have passed since this awful tragedy transpired, I don't remember all of the details. I do remember being at the funeral and that some of my colleagues were there too. Later in the year, the staff decided to plant a tree in memory of the girls' father and a small ceremony was to be held after school one day. I seem to recall that our principal was sick that day, but it wasn't appropriate to cancel the event just because of her illness. Shannon no longer was attending our school and was now in junior high. I remember the school counselor, one other teacher, the head custodian, Shannon and Sharon, and perhaps a couple of their close friends attending. I suspect the principal would have said a few words if she were there that day, but after the counselor spoke, she asked if anyone else wanted to share any words. I remember that there was a very uncomfortable silence, and I suddenly felt the need to say something and be supportive to the girls because the atmosphere was so sad. I didn't really know what kind of ceremony we were having that day, but I somehow tried to find the right words at that particular moment to be comforting and supportive.

Being a teacher is only one of the many roles we take on. I played the role of nurse, disciplinarian, counselor, advocate, parent, role model, and even friend. While some of the things you deal with as a teacher repeat themselves year after year and become familiar, sometimes you are suddenly thrust into a different role because of unusual circumstances.

On one occasion, I recall that I was teaching a combination 5th -6th- grade level class, and two of my students had been in the girls' bathroom together. Suddenly, one of the girls, "Laura," came running into class showing immediate concern and panic. She told me that her classmate, "Julie," had turned pale and collapsed in the bathroom. I never before had left my class unattended; this seemed like a real emergency, so I hurriedly went to the restroom. That was the only time in my career that I went barging into the girls' bathroom, but considering the circumstances, it seemed like the only thing to do. Sure enough, I found Julie crumpled up and laying on the floor. She was breathing but nearly unconscious when I arrived. I quickly scooped her up in my arms and carried her to the office. Next to the office was a room for ill students with a type of cot in it. I laid my student down, and the secretary took over at that point.

I quickly dashed back to my class, and the other kids were in an understandable state of bewilderment and concern. At that point, I didn't know what the circumstances were, but I had to try to ease their understandable fear for their classmate while feeling upset myself. There was nothing in my teacher training that would have prepared me for a situation like this, and all that I could tell the kids was that the secretary was caring for her now and that she was in good hands. The class had as many questions as I did, and yet I had to try to reassure them and somehow get back to some semblance of learning. It, fortunately, turned out to be just a scary situation rather than anything serious. Julie had inadvertently cut her finger somehow, and the sight of her blood had frightened her to the point that she began going into shock.

For several years, we had class pets in my room. I had a pair of rats for much of this time. Some of the children were pretty squeamish around them initially, but as the year went on, most of the kids overcame that fear and came to like them. One of the class jobs was to clean the pen, feed them daily, and provide fresh water for them whenever they needed it. I had to put the cage in the back of the classroom away from the kids for the majority of the day, or they would become distracted. Lots of days I had the rat cage out on the floor where the kids could observe them before school. Rats don't live an unusually long life (2-3 years), and the first time my pair passed away was in the summer.

I can't say that I ever got attached to those little guys the way the kids did, but having any animal in your classroom can be kind of risky. For one thing, there was always the worry about what to do if one of the pets passed away. Another obvious concern was what to do with the animals on vacations and weekends. One consideration was thinking about the possibility of the pets escaping in the classroom. These issues were all things I eventually had to deal with at one time or another in my class. On one occasion, one of the rats passed away during the middle of school, and the child who found him announced this sad news to the class. All of the other kids wanted to know if it was true and tried to gather around the cage. I tried to protect the kids from any unnecessary pain, so I just decided to move the pen out of sight and told them perhaps the rat was just sick. I reassured them that I would take it to the veterinarian after school.

Of course, when I investigated after they had left, I confirmed the rat was no longer alive. I called the school counselor and asked for some advice on what to do. Fortunately, she had a book about the death of a pet, and she suggested I read that to the class and then take it from there. I'd dealt with some sad things like this before, and the kids, quite naturally, were trying to process it all. I know I've had students who have had a pet pass away and then wanted to share this with their classmates. That can be a very tricky situation though. You realize that it is important for the children to express their feelings and you want to be supportive, but what inevitably happened was that other children wanted to share about a time when their animal passed away. Predictably, this would lead to one of the kids having sad thoughts, and the tears would start. That, in turn, would lead to other kids getting upset, and then I'd feel awful for having gone down this road in the first place.

In the case of the passing rat, I read the book that the counselor gave me. Instead of letting the kids express their feelings aloud, I put on some instrumental music and allowed them to write or make a card if they wanted to. All of a sudden, I had kids who were asking if we could bring the rat cage out and have them present their cards to the remaining rat. As I said before, sometimes you have to trust your instincts about what to do in a classroom. There was no handbook for situations like these when they arose. Hopefully, you make the right decisions and do what is best for your students. Many of my students wanted to present their cards to the remaining rat, and I took an edu-cated risk and allowed this to happen. What ensued was the one and only rat memorial at my school. The kids showed their cards to the rest of the class if they wanted to. I even had a couple of kids in the class who made cards for me, thinking that I would be devastated by the death of one of the class pets. The irony here was that I was wor-ried about my students and trying to let them process the passing of a class pet and grieve to some degree so that we could move on, and yet some kids were worried about me. It was so incredibly sweet!

There were times in my career when the unexpected event could turn heartbreaking too. One such occasion occurred near the end of a typical school day. Our school is in a residential neighborhood, and many of the kids lived close. There was a family whose house was within view of the front of the school and the playground. Four kids from this family passed through our school. Many of these kids were problematic because they could be behavior problems, and their work habits were poor. Their dad was in and out of jail, and we only had contact with the mother over the years. She was at our school a lot since her children were frequently in trouble. There often was a re-entry meeting between the principal, teacher, parent(s), and student when a child was about to return from a suspension. The tone of these meetings varied from situation to situation. The meeting was not so much a focus on what occurred, but an attempt to come up with a plan as to how we were going to try and work together to avoid any future problems. Many times the school would learn about family issues during these meetings. Quite often there was a certain amount of upheaval within the family which may have accounted, in part, for a child acting out in school.

On this particular day, I was outside with my class taking part in physical education with them. For many kids, this was their favorite part of the day, and I also looked forward to it. As I was supervising a game my students were playing, three police cars pulled up abruptly in front of the house across the street. The officers ran up to the house, and my instinct was to immediately bring my class inside because I wasn't sure if this was a potentially dangerous situation. A lot of the kids in my class were curious about what was going on, but the child who was most concerned was "Travis." He was a 6th grader and the third oldest child of the four kids. I remember that he didn't want to go back into the classroom, and his eyes focused on the activity that was taking place at his home. It was one of those situations where I suddenly needed an additional adult to help because I had a classroom of kids ready to re-enter my room and a student who refused to move, standing like a statue, in the middle of the field. Travis's actions, or lack thereof, in this case, seemed to be based more on curiosity rather than defiance. I couldn't imagine what was going through his head as he watched intently. I sent one of my students to the office to try to get some help, and I went to talk to him again.

After what seemed to be an interminable amount of time, he reluctantly came into class with the rest of us. The student who I had sent to the office returned saying that the principal was in a meeting and couldn't come. The other thing that made this a challenging situation is that many other kids in the class wanted to know what was going on and didn't realize that Travis lived at this house. The kids had lots of questions about what was happening, and I didn't have any answers for them. There were thirty minutes left in the school day, so I decided to put on a movie to try to distract them from what was occurring. You could see Travis's house from my classroom. I shut the curtains, and most of the kids became engaged in the movie, but Travis just stood at the back of the room peeking around the curtains. It was a helpless feeling as his teacher because I wanted to comfort and reassure him that everything would be alright. I walked back to him during the movie, and I could see the situation was still in progress. About that time, the police came out of the house and had Travis's dad in handcuffs. I felt horrible for Travis as a tear slowly began rolling down his cheek. I wished that I could somehow comfort him, but there was nothing that I could say at that point that would make it better. He finally returned to his seat, and he just put his head down, and he began weeping softly.

Finally, my principal showed up to our classroom, and I explained to her privately what was going on. She went over to Travis and talked to him quietly and got him to leave with her. Of course, the other kids in the class were all wanting to know what was going on. In general, I believe in being honest with kids. The problem was, in this particular situation, I felt this student's privacy took priority over their natural curiosity. I didn't know everything about what was going on anyway, so I just kept telling them, "I don't know." It was one of those tough situations that you face as a teacher from time to time. I don't even know, to this day, if I would have done anything differently because sometimes there is no easy answer when it comes to situations like this. It was just a trying experience.

Some of the most memorable students in my class were the ones who were a little different from their classmates. We all have our oddities and peculiarities, but that is what makes us individuals. While some older children will call a classmate "weird" when they act a little differently, I preferred to refer to these children as "unique," which has a much more positive connotation. Part of my responsibility as a teacher was to have my students respect everyone as an individual. I tried to teach my children that we are diverse in many ways and that none of them should feel ashamed if they acted or dressed in a manner that was dissimilar to other people. In fact, this might even lead to a discussion of how many people have come to America with different backgrounds, and how we should respect and celebrate their uniqueness. Sometimes these differences have nothing to do with being from another country or part of another culture.

In a 5th grade class I had a boy named "Jeff." One of the issues I had with him throughout the year was that he was girl crazy. He was a very likable kid. He had some learning disabilities, but that hardly should affect the way anyone thought of him. I did have to tell him to cool it with the girls from time to time.

At some point in the year, I began receiving complaints from some of the girls in the room who told me he was approaching them at recess and asking them if they wanted to kiss him. I remember pulling him aside at recess one day and telling him that he was not to proposition the girls in this manner.

He seemed to understand and said very seriously, "I'll try not to do that anymore, Mr. Springer. I want you to know that I'm going to try, but I can't promise you anything because they are so pretty!"

Well, I appreciated his honesty, and he did refrain from harassing the girls after that. At the end of the year, we had an annual talent show. I use the term "talent" quite loosely because some of the acts are anything but talented. In elementary school, the talent show was one of those things that often became a source of controversy. Most of the drama occurred because some of the kids, and even parents, would take this so seriously and kind of boss or bully other kids. Children were going in and out of acts all the time depending on who wanted to practice at recess. That, of course, led to a series of disagreements where kids argued about who was in and who was out of their act. Some of the 6th-grade girls, in particular, were not so nice to each other during this time. Not only were there disagreements about who was going to perform in the group, but it sometimes evolved to the point where they might put down somebody else's act. I remember having to counsel kids about how to manage these interpersonal relationships during the lead-up to the talent show so they could remain friends.

During this particular year, Jeff wanted to sing a song, but he wanted to have a partner for his performance. He had developed quite a reputation over the years for some of his singing performances. Jeff wasn't a bad singer, but the songs that he chose to sing were often not popular, mainstream songs. For about two weeks he tried to find a partner in the class to do his song with, but most of the kids thought his song was weird. The song that he chose to perform this particular year was called <u>One Eyed, One Horned, Flying Purple People Eater</u>. I could tell he was feeling discouraged that no one in the class wanted to do the song with him. I felt sad for him because he put his heart and soul into his singing performances, and I told him that I would do the song with him. Of course, I didn't even know what I was volunteering for at the time, but I soon found out. Jeff's grandma made costumes for both of us, and he brought in a CD so that I could learn the song. We even did a little choreography because the song needed something. In the end, we performed together, and the kids and the staff thoroughly enjoyed our act.

I recall a time when the principal shared a letter that a parent had written to the school. She was not a student of mine, but once again I was reminded of the impact that teachers/administrators can have on their students. The woman, now an adult, had written a letter to the school telling of a valuable lesson she had learned. I don't remember the exact details, but the letter described that at one point she had taken $2.00 from a teacher's desk at school when she was a child. She realized at the time she had done something that was wrong, but she didn't know, as a child, what to do to make it right. The letter went on to tell that she was now a mother and had a daughter who she loved and to whom she was trying to teach a valuable lesson. She apologized and sent $3.00 back (including $1.00 for accrued interest) to the school because she wanted to demonstrate to her daughter about taking responsibility for your actions. Even though this wasn't one of my students, it made a powerful impression on me at the time and has remained locked away in my memory bank through the years.

Another example of being unaware of the powerful impact that we sometimes are having on our students was reinforced years ago by another former student. My wife has a good friend, "Sandy." She lived in a nearby city and had come across a young married lady named "Monique." Somehow the subject of favorite teachers came up, and Monique told Sandy that her favorite teacher growing up was a Mr. Springer. I remembered teaching Monique in 5th or 6th grade. (I taught both classes separately and sometimes together). She was a good student with a lively personality, but there was nothing in my memory of her that would suggest to me that I'd have been her favorite teacher. In fact, I would never have even known about this if my wife wasn't close friends with Sandy today. When Sandy heard this story about me being Monique's favorite teacher, she thoughtfully passed it on to my wife who relayed it to me.

The compelling message that I want to impart to anyone in the teaching profession is, "What we do matters!" Teaching is one of those professions that gives us the opportunity to make a difference in our students' lives. I am a pretty easygoing guy for the most part, but I get bent out of shape when I hear education and teachers being badmouthed by individuals who have no idea of the difficult circumstances with which most teachers have to contend. Teaching, like any profession, has a few bad apples, but the majority of teachers are talented and generous people who give their all every day to help their students.

I'd like to close this chapter with a story that happened during my last year of teaching. One of my co-workers has a daughter named "Gwen." I first got to know Gwen when she came into my sixth-grade class in the middle of the year. I believe she had not been doing very well at her previous school. Having a little background information is nice, but it also shouldn't influence the way teachers treat any of their students. You have to have an open mind because everyone deserves a fresh start. My experience with Gwen was not a particularly memorable one. I recall her as being a very cooperative student who did everything that I asked. She quickly made new friends, and she was more mature than the typical sixth grader. I found her to be a wonderful student, and I enjoyed being her teacher.

Years later she came back to our school and worked as a member of the support staff. She left the school, got married and started a family at some point. I would occasionally see her over the years when she came back to see her mom (also employed at my school) or when she was working around town.

The last couple of years of my career she came back to our school and did many different jobs around campus. She worked in the cafeteria, classroom, did bus duty, and worked in the after-school program. Her story was not that different from many young people, including me when I was much younger. She was still searching for what she wanted to do in her life.

She was working in my room during reading group, and she was very good with the kids. I could see that she possessed a lot of natural skills as a leader and disciplinarian. She genuinely cared about the kids, and I saw her potential as a teacher. The kids also liked and respected her. Near the end of the school year, I was pleasantly surprised when she left me the nicest card, and said that I had inspired her and that she had decided to go back to school with the ultimate goal of becoming a teacher. After school ended and I was cleaning out my classroom for the last time before retirement, I threw away a lot of stuff or tried to give it away to my colleagues. I did keep a lot of things for Gwen though, and when the day comes, I have this vision of passing on these resources and helping her set up her first classroom. I feel like a proud papa after watching my former student grow into a leader, and I am so glad to see her working her way toward her goal of becoming a teacher.

Funny Moments at School

A good sense of humor is essential for a teacher or anyone working in a school. While I wouldn't have traded all the crazy moments of my career as a teacher for anything, I do know that one way I dealt with the constant pressures and stresses of the job was to laugh. Teaching is never boring! I started each day knowing that something I had never experienced before might happen that day. Some of the things that happened were so absurd that I still laugh about them today.

You have to be prepared to fill so many roles when you work at a school, particularly when you are an elementary school teacher. One year the school nurse asked if I would take on the job of sex education teacher for the 6th-grade boys. The nurse said that she would take my 6th-grade girls but preferred to have a male do the boys' presentation. She must have caught me at a weak moment because I asked her what the job entailed. She gave me the lowdown.

I would be showing the boys a movie about the changes that take place with boys and girls during puberty and then have a discussion with them and answer their questions. I could preview the movie ahead of time before I committed to doing this. I remember taking the movie home and watching it. It seemed to be tastefully done, and I reluctantly agreed. Sex education was not always looked upon with approval by parents. They had time to review the materials with the school nurse if they wanted to see what the kids were going to learn. Parents had to be notified ahead of time and give their consent. If they did not want their child to participate, the kids went to another classroom during the presentation.

From previous years, I remembered the kind of nervous excitement the kids had on sex education day. I'm sure they were experiencing a lot of different feelings when this day finally arrived. Most of the kids generally got permission to attend, but there was an awkwardness for the kids who didn't receive permission. The nurse departed with the girls, and I suddenly was left with the mixture of sweaty and smelly guys who thought they were going to learn about the secrets of girls from their experienced and nervous teacher.

One of the things that I had been instructed to do by the nurse was to leave a can out on my desk with an opportunity for the boys to put in anonymous questions for me to address following the movie. The can remained empty in the days leading up to the presentation. Who really wanted to be the kid who strode purposefully forward in front of his classmates and submitted an inquiry when everyone else would know it was his question? I'm sure there were a mixture of kids who wanted everyone to think they knew all about this already, and those that didn't want to come across like they were some kind of pervert by asking questions in the first place. There also was a segment of boys who probably had little interest in this topic yet.

I was also instructed to give each boy an index card and have him jot down any questions that he might have during the movie. The kids who didn't have any questions were told to write "I have no questions" on their card.

After the movie I was to lead a discussion about kids caring for their hygiene. I did this presentation three years in a row, and what usually transpired was that there was dead silence in the room unless one student was brave enough to ask a question. I then would go through the index cards and the majority of them would say, "I have no questions." I'd finish looking through the cards and realize there were thirty more minutes of time before the girls were scheduled to return. (The girls' sessions always seemed to go much longer than the boys.) With little discussion taking place, it was only logical to end it and ask the boys if they wanted to go out early for P.E. Of course, they did! They had survived the dreaded sex education day and got extra P.E. as an added bonus!

The last year I did the boys' presentation, it was considerably different. As I looked at the index cards, there were a couple of them that were loaded with questions. I don't mean just any questions either. These were the kind of questions that I was turning five shades of red just reading. There was no way that I would or could even attempt to answer some of their very specific sexual questions.

After this experience, I decided it was going to have to be someone else's job to educate my boys because their teacher wasn't up to the task. The girls came back to class at the end of the day feeling equally embarrassed, as if they had just learned some deep, dark secrets. It was at that moment I decided that sex education was something that I wasn't going to be doing again anytime soon.

When I first started as a teacher, I was nervous about having parent-teacher conferences. It was something new for me, and I wanted to put my best foot forward. One valuable part of my student teaching experience was that sometimes my master teacher would invite me to sit in on the conferences and asked me to contribute any additional information that I might have. I welcomed this practical experience and found it much more valuable than many of my teaching prep classes I took in college, which focused more on theory.

Once I started holding my conferences, I realized that many of the parents were more nervous than I. Our school held parent-teacher conferences after school. All of those conference days were minimum days, and then we would have a week to power through all of the conferences. That week was pretty challenging, primarily when I taught upper elementary school, as those classes had more children. I remember getting through five or six conferences and then realizing it was past 5:00 p.m., and I had yet to invest one minute of time in preparation for the following school day. At one point, California adopted a class size reduction policy, and I often had only twenty students in the 2nd or 3rd grade. Having taught in grades 4th-6th for many years with classes that may have contained ten or more students than the primary grades, I know that this was one of those inequities that bothered the upper elementary teachers.

While I was enrolled in college, I was working part-time in various elementary schools as a teacher's aide for about four years. One year I worked in a resource room and special day class for students with learning problems. The teacher in the resource room had the foresight to have me take part in the parent-teacher conferences. That was my first experience with conferences, and there was one time I had to do everything in my power to keep from bursting out in laughter during the meeting.

The teacher was discussing with the parent about the lack of self-control of his son, especially on the playground where the boy frequently lost his cool and started in with profanities toward other students and sometimes at the supervisors. The teacher was talking about how her student would have time-outs when this occurred, and then the parent responded in complete seriousness with one of the all-time classic lines, "Yeah, I don't know where in the hell he gets that goddamn, son of a bitch language from!" It was a line you might hear in a comedy movie, but that was about the last thing I expected to hear at a conference. The fact that the parent was so oblivious made it all the more priceless.

One would think that parents would also want to put their best foot forward at these conferences too, but it was quite surprising when, on occasion, I would meet a parent who came in drunk, high, or under the influence of something. Some were shockingly honest and told me things like, "Well, his dad has to get him up in the morning because I am an exotic dancer, and I work late hours. Sometimes his dad gets drunk, and we all sleep in."

I don't mean to make light of these kinds of comments, but the reality is that some of your students are coming to school from these types of environments. One teacher I taught with tells a story of how he was conducting a parent-teacher conference with his 6th grade student and the boy's parents. The dad, inexplicably, chose that moment to present his wife with divorce papers. What do you do in a completely unexpected situation like that? The teacher pulled the boy out of the room in the middle of the conference to go shoot some baskets with him and said to the parents, "I'm going to leave you here because it seems like you have some things to get worked out."

Since I taught for so many years in the same school, one of the strangest experiences was to sit down and have a parent-teacher conference with a parent who used to be one of my students. In fact, this experience happened several times to me near the end of my career. Besides the obvious physical similarities that are passed on from generation to generation, I also saw some connections with personality traits shared between parent and child. I remember having a parent conference with one of my former students, and I was telling the parent that the child had a hard time staying focused and quite often was out of his seat.

In fact, the child reminded me of his dad who was precisely the same way when I had taught him nearly twenty years before. Some of my colleagues and I used to joke with one another about the kinds of things we really would like to say in the circumstances like this. Somehow, I restrained myself from saying, "Your child is quite a pain in the butt! In fact, he reminds me a lot of you when you were in my class!"

There were so many times we did crazy things as a staff at school. We often did a performance at the end of the year talent show. Not all of the teachers would participate, but everyone was welcome to join in. One of my colleagues would often come up with some song for us to learn, including choreographed dance moves too. Her daughter was a high school cheerleading coach and sometimes even tried to help us develop our routine. I'm sure at some point her daughter felt like saying, "What did I get myself into with this sorry group?"

There was nothing quite as funny to me as watching somebody who is uncool (teachers from a different generation) trying to be cool. We did all kinds of musical performances including country, rock, disco, and even hip-hop. We would go all out, including getting costumes for whatever kind of song that we were performing. I remember one year being the Blues Brothers with one of my colleagues. My funniest recollection was when the teachers tried to rap. I don't even remember what the song was, but it was truly hilarious being so out of our element as we "rapped" to our own beats. I had such a hard time learning my lines that I had mine written on my hand. Sometimes our performances were videotaped and ended up on YouTube. During our performance you could see me staring at my hand intently as if in some kind of trance.

One of the other teachers would introduce us and get the kids all worked up, telling them that the school had flown in these well-known performers at great expense. Most of the kids had seen this before, and the only mystery was what new depths of humiliation we would reach in this year's performance. By the time we finished, the kids in the audience were thoroughly whipped up into a frenzy of craziness.

When my son was in 6th grade, I wanted to do something with him in the talent show before he moved on to junior high. I wrote a silly skit about us being newscasters together. We even went to a local car dealership and borrowed the soundtrack to their radio/television jingle so that we could have a commercial during the "newscast." When the "newscasters" whipped out their rubber guitars and completely got into their roles as rock stars, it made for quite a father/son memory. That was one of my happiest and silliest memories of teaching because I got to share the spotlight with my son.

Some of the funniest moments occurred when kids didn't intend to be funny. I wish I would have written down all of the spelling errors and humor that kids inadvertently created in their writing because there were so many. Sometimes when I was alone in my living room correcting papers in the evening, I would come across spelling or grammar errors that were so bad that they were priceless. Children inadvertently replaced the intended words with other words that changed the meaning entirely and led to some late-night entertainment for me. There was the reversal of letters that led to some classics:

"Where did that ditch come from?" became, "Where did that bitch come from?" Simply getting one letter wrong turned "My uncle wants a big deck" into "My uncle wants a big dick." Adding the wrong letter to a sentence changed the meaning completely as in, "The coach wanted to know if anyone found a red cap in the dugout after the last game," was mistakenly written as "The coach wanted to know if anyone found a red crap in the dugout after the last game." I know there were many others, but those are some of the funniest ones I can still remember off the top of my head.

Then there were the most memorable excuses that my 5th and 6th grade students gave me for not having their homework:

#5 Somebody broke into my dad's car last night and stole my backpack. **(Math papers are a hot item with thieves these days.)**

#4 My mom forgot to make me do it. **(She's really been falling down on the job lately.)**

#3 My parents made me go to the movies with them so I didn't have time. **(Why didn't they make me? I would have liked a night off too.)**

#2 My parents don't allow us to do homework on "Family Game Night." **(Good to know that they've got their priorities in order.)**

#1 I thought you were kidding. **(Yes, this sounds exactly like the kind of thing I'd joke about.)**

Sometimes situations that seemed scary at the time turned out to be pretty funny later. When I first started teaching we only practiced fire drills and the occasional earthquake drill. One of the sad realities of life is that with increased levels of violence in society, we needed to start practicing drills that involved lockdowns.

At one time our doors only had locks on the outside. I pictured the scene where I would be fumbling with my keys while somebody with bad intentions stood by waiting for me to get the door locked. Not too realistic! Thankfully, this is one of the reasons we have drills because you learn how ill-prepared you are. In a lockdown, the teacher quickly locks all the doors to his/her classroom, shuts the curtains, and turns off the lights. Depending on the circumstances of the drill, we sometimes had the kids gather around the teacher on the floor in a corner away from the doors. During many drills, the kids and teacher would have to try and get under a desk. I'm sure there was nothing more comical for the kids than to watch their overweight teacher trying to fit under a tiny desk, but I felt like it was our duty to lead by example.

At the start of the school year our school administrator would give us an advanced warning for when a drill was going to occur. That way you could forewarn the kids and practice the routines that they needed to learn. I would occasionally get younger students who were frightened, even though I told them in advance that we would have a drill at 10:00 and what we would be doing. As kids got better trained, the administrator would occasionally have an unannounced drill, and even the teacher might not know if an event was real or practice.

On one memorable occasion, we had to crawl under our desks when the administrator got on the phone and announced we were having a "shelter in place." I did not know anything about the drill, and the kids immediately began questioning if it was practice or real. During a "shelter in place" everyone is supposed to be very quiet, so I immediately called for the kids to be silent. As we were all crouched under our desks in uncomfortable fetal positions, there suddenly was a noise outside our door, and we heard the sound of someone try-ing to enter the room. There was an audible gasp from some of my students who were frightened. To make the situation even scarier, the person continued to grab the handle and attempted to open the door. The kids feared the worst, and I was concerned as well.

I suddenly had a feeling that perhaps one of my students had showed up late and may have been trying to enter the room. I crawled out from under my desk and made my way toward the door. One of the kids in my class even called out, "No!" in fear that I might be preparing to let in the intruder. As I got close to the door, I peered through the small vertical window in the door and saw a student from another class trying to figure out what to do with this locked door. I could not understand why he would be trying to enter our room during a drill, but my curious nature told me to see why he was there. When I opened the door, he handed me a stack of papers. During this year, two of my colleagues and I had been switching classes during math time. The student who was at the door was merely there to hand me the homework papers from my math students ahead of time.

It was only later, at break time, that I learned that my colleague was unaware that we were even holding a drill, as his class did not hear the warning in his classroom. Things like that demonstrate why you need to have practiced so that you can iron out all of the bugs before an actual emergency occurs.

At times, kids create humor without really intending to. I wish that I had a dollar for every time that I was called "Mom" by one of my students. That is something that happened every year, especially with the younger children. It was always said unintentionally. Most times the student would sheepishly laugh, realizing it sounded funny to be calling his/her male teacher, "Mom." Instead of being some-how offended, I took this as a wonderful compliment. The idea that a teacher was like a mom to a child was a very nice comparison, even if it was said by accident. However, I could not account for why they called me "mom" more than they called me "dad." I'll leave it to someone else to figure that one out. I even was called "grandma" by one of my students one day. I remember telling my student in a joking manner, "If I look like your grandma, then one of us (either grandma or me) has a problem."

While I enjoyed taking field trips, there was always a part of me that was relieved when we returned to school without any incident. One year I was teaching 2nd grade, and my class attended a field trip with another 2nd grade class from my school. When you are a teach-er, you have to learn all the tricks of the trade. One of those tricks was that we were usually allowed to take more field trips if we went with other classrooms. So many decisions made in a school are based on economics, and field trips were no different.

There were years when we were allowed to only take one field trip, and I recall another year when we weren't permitted to take any.

It was more cost-effective for a bus to take two classes on the same day as opposed to taking each class on separate days. On this particular field trip, my teaching colleague and I decided to take our 2nd graders to the local zoo. To make this more manageable for the zoo and also for us, there was a period when one class was touring the zoo and visiting the animals while the other group was being shown a video and listening to a presentation. We had many parent chaperones along on this day, and it was much more practical to have each parent look after three or four kids than try to keep the entire class in one spot together. At the end of the field trip, we all got back on the bus, and my colleague and I were making final head counts to ensure that everyone was accounted for. My colleague suddenly became alarmed when she realized that one of her students was missing.

At first, you assume that there is a logical explanation. Perhaps one of the kids went to the bathroom, and the chaperone somehow got distracted and forgot about the child. She took attendance again and realized that the child was really missing. Of course, we didn't want to alarm the kids and other adults unnecessarily, but I'm sure a bit of panic began to come over us. A few parents stayed on the bus with the bus driver and the rest of the class. A group of three of us (the two teachers and one other parent) went to scour the grounds looking for the missing child. Five minutes later the child was found sitting in the petting zoo, focusing her attention on the goats and other small animals. She was contentedly petting the animals, oblivious that her group had left. How the chaperone failed to notice that this child wasn't with their small group was hard to fathom, but that was one day I'll never forget.

There was no shortage of adventure when we had a field trip to the swimming pool. Most kids loved this field trip, but very seldom did it go off without a hitch. Trying to manage sometimes as many as sixty kids in the pool and locker room was a challenge. The kids were so excited that they just wanted to get out to the pool. The pool staff tried different things over the years to help children keep track of their belongings, but whatever they did, we always seemed to end up with one or more children who couldn't find their clothes when it was time to get dressed. Nearly every year we took this trip, practically all the kids were showered and dressed, sitting on the bus, while we waited for someone to find a missing article of clothing. No matter how many times I had the kids put their clothes in a locker, their backpack, or the bags which were hanging in the dressing area, something always went missing. I'd be in the dressing room trying to prod the boys along. Without fail, some child would call out, "I can't find my underwear," or "My shirt isn't here!" The pool staff helped us out more than once by providing some student with an old article of clothing that another child had previously left behind.

I remember one day after school following a field trip when one of my student's parents called and asked me if I knew where "Robert's" underwear was. Was she honestly asking me this question? Did she think perhaps that I wanted to keep his underwear as a souvenir? I would get off the phone after one of these conversations and ask myself, "Am I dreaming, or did that just happen?"

My favorite regular field trip was whenever I took my kids and some of their parents on a bike ride to a neighboring park. I usually did this the week before school was out, and it was a very fun and exciting way to culminate the year. In knowing how cautious schools are, in general, about avoiding potential liability, I was amazed at the number of years the administration allowed me to take this trip. In all the years that I took my class, I never had one serious incident occur. It was a very well-orchestrated event though. We rode in a long, single file formation, and I always interspersed parent bike riders throughout the line. At busy intersections, I had a parent stationed to act as a crossing guard, and we would get off our bikes and cross the street carefully. I also had parents driving their vehicles in front of and behind our group with their flashers on. If a student had a mechanical issue with a bike, there was always somebody right there to help the child. Kids who got tired or were unable to ride the whole way could get a ride with one of the parents who were driving a truck in the back of the group. The preplanning for this day took quite a bit of time because the school required the parents to show proof of insurance and have their vehicle inspected ahead of time in the event that they might be transporting a child.

When I took this trip with 2nd or 3rd graders, there were times a child or two hadn't learned to ride a bike yet, and so I had to make sure that they could all ride safely in the first place. Four miles was plenty of riding for 2nd and 3rd graders, but I did ten-mile trips for kids in 5th and 6th grades. We'd stop at a designated spot along the way to get a drink and have a short rest before continuing. Once we got to the park we played games between the parents/kids, ate lunch together (either BBQed hot dogs or pizza), had some kind of performance by the kids for the parents, and closed the day with awards.

In addition to recognizing individual achievements, I often gave each student in my class a medal stating how many Accelerated Reader* points they had earned for the school year. (*Accelerated Reader is a program in which students read books and then take assessments on the computer. The kids earn points based on the difficulty of the book and how well they do on the accompanying comprehension test.) This day was usually the kids' favorite school day of the year. I liked it too because it always brought a smile to my face to see them so happy and to be able to enjoy this field trip with their parents. One remarkable year, every child in the class had a parent come along with us for this field trip!

Finally, my administrator told me that I could no longer take this trip. I understood his concern because there were always unforeseen circumstances that could happen. For one, a child could possibly fall and get seriously hurt. Certainly, a child could run into a parked car or another bike rider. At times we would come across a loose dog, and there was the potential for a child to be bitten or panic and fall if the child saw the dog as a threat. When I was told that I could no longer take my biking trip, there was a part of me that was sad. Like many teachers though, I tried to move to Plan B when something did not go my way. The administrator's biggest concern was the riding of bicycles away from campus and the potential for some kind of accident to occur. With my administrator's approval, we began holding the event at school and did everything we did before with the exception of riding our bikes. Sure, the kids missed that part, but in my eyes, it was better to adjust the plan than to scrap it altogether. This event started out as something fun I did with my own class, but when it got moved to our school, my grade level colleagues wanted to be included too. I understood this completely because I'm sure their students were asking them, "Why can't we do this too?"

The last few years we pulled it off at school with our three third grade classes altogether. Between all of the kids and parents who attended, we usually had to buy twenty-five extra-large pizzas. I know kids well enough to know that these are the kinds of things they will remember forever when they think back to their elementary years. I had a 3rd grade colleague who retired several years before me who used to take her class on a camping trip for a few days. I know that two fifth grade teachers at our sister school take an end-of-the-year trip. Individual sacrifices like this happen all the time among teachers, but these events are memorable.

When I taught 6th grade, one of my colleagues and I took our classes to a state campground for three days and two nights that was about forty-five minutes away. That was something we planned as a culmination of their elementary school experience. We tried to be very busy during the day and took part in a lot of hiking and physical activities, mainly because we wanted the kids tired when bedtime rolled around. We often rented a group campground and would organize the kids in gender groups. They put up their own tents in a semi-circular pattern. Part of the overall experience was just seeing if the kids could figure out how to work together to put up their group tent.

As it was not appropriate to be in the same tent as any of my students, I would either go to sleep in the back of my pickup or set up my own individual tent near the kids. Taking a group of kids camping was an enormous responsibility, and I never slept that well when I was on one of these trips. By the end of the day, I was pretty exhausted. Most nights I would have a very restless sleep, waking up to each little noise and movement. Periodically, I get very intense leg cramps, and they often occur in the middle of the night when I roll over in bed and change positions.

The pain from these is nearly unbearable, and some nights at home I am flopping around on the floor like a fish out of water because it hurts so much. If I can straighten my leg out, the pain usually starts to subside after a minute or so. If you've never had one of these, consider yourself lucky because they rank among the most painful physical experiences that I've ever had. When I'm having a leg cramp, the muscles in my leg are so taut that they look like they are going to come through my skin. While I never swore in front of any of my students before, I remember being in my tent one night and getting one of these incredibly painful leg cramps. I wanted to scream out and let loose with a string of profanities, but I had enough awareness of where I was to avoid doing so. My only recourse was to bite on my pillow as hard as I could while trying not to flop around too much. The next day one of the kids in the neighboring tent asked me if something had happened to me in the middle of the night because he apparently heard me thrashing about.

There are times I look back and question what we could possibly have been thinking. For a few years we held an annual sleepover at school for the kids who had achieved some reading goal. For some reason, we decided to hold this event on a Thursday night at school. There would be somewhere in the neighborhood of twenty to twenty-five kids most years. In the late afternoon, we played some outdoor games with the kids. This was typically followed by a pizza dinner, and then we separated the kids by gender into two different rooms before bedtime. The kids would unroll their sleeping bags, make themselves comfortable, and then we'd put on a movie in each room. When it got late, we turned out the lights and all went to sleep. At least, that was the plan. These nights, sleeping on a hard floor with a bunch of kids at school, rank right up there with the worst nights of sleep I've ever had! Some kids felt restless (perhaps a little homesickness) and others were talking in their sleep all night. If that wasn't crazy enough, in the morning we had to feed the kids breakfast and then get ready to teach. I can recall thinking at the time as I was shaving and then shampooing my hair in the sink at school the following morning that this had to be the definition of insanity. Events like this were voluntary for the staff to take part in, but I always felt a sense of obligation and desire to show kids that we were there to support and guide them.

Another comical experience happened when a student was having a sleepover at his house and invited some classmates. This was not that odd, but what was strange was that he handed me an invitation too. I did not go, but for years after that when I was meeting parents on Back to School Night, I would tell them how I tried to attend an extracurricular activity of each of my students, but I could promise them that I wouldn't be attending any sleepovers.

If you are going to be a teacher, there are probably going to be occasions when you end up looking back and reminiscing about doing something that you would never have imagined yourself doing. I have lots of these memories. Some involve crazy things that we would do together as a staff. A tradition started in which we dressed up following some kind of theme for Halloween. We often tried to come up with something with which the kids would be somewhat familiar. One time we dressed as school supplies, and I actually made a costume where I was a box of tissue. That year I got very creative and painted and stenciled a box that could fit over my body. My wife and I cut a slit for a small opening, and I taped a real container of Kleenex inside my large box. That way the students could grab a tissue directly from me. One year we dressed as characters from the animated kids' film, <u>Toy Story</u>. Another year we were characters from the old movie, <u>The Wizard of Oz</u>. The biggest challenge became just coming up with an idea that was practical, inexpensive enough to pull off, and agreeable to all the staff members.

Around school, there usually are a lot of days when the kids and the staff dress up. Besides the usual dressing up for Halloween, there were several other dress-up days including dressing up as a favorite book character, a worker for a particular career, a school spirit day, and countless other things.

One day we had something called Backward Day at school. Kids and staff members did things like wearing shirts and hats backward. Never one to shy away from things like that, I remember wearing my underwear over my pants and my socks on my hands. When I look back at those kinds of things now, I have to laugh and shake my head in amazement that I did that. You can't be shy and embarrassed if you're going to be a teacher.

While there are certain behaviors and things I dealt with every year as a teacher, there were also those moments when something brand new would happen. Sometimes these events were scary, touching, or even humorous. I once had a 2nd grade boy in my class who had a couple of older brothers involved in athletics. "Ted" had seen his brothers celebrating with a teammate when they made a touchdown by chest bumping. If you aren't familiar with this celebration, it involves two teammates leaping into the air simultaneously and purposely hitting their chests together as a symbol of celebration. I had seen it before at different sporting events, otherwise I would have been totally confused.

I normally greeted and said goodbye to each of my students at the start and end of each school day. One day as I was saying goodbye, Ted suddenly leaped up and gave me a chest bump. I was so surprised I didn't even know how to react, but I could not help laughing because it must have been a comical sight. Ted was probably the smallest child in the class, and I was six feet tall and weighed two hundred and fifty pounds at the time. Not once in my teacher training classes did the subject of students chest bumping the teacher ever come up. Oh well, I looked at things like that as what made the job interesting because something out of the ordinary happened all the time. Since the other students laughed so hard that day, Ted decided to repeat himself the next day. While he really was just having a bit of fun, I decided after day two that I better put a stop to this, or I would probably end up with a whole bunch of kids following suit. I doubt my principal at the time would have found this as humorous as I did.

Another year my fifth-grade girls decided to play a joke on me for April Fool's Day. I got wind of it right away because a couple of the boys came in before school and told me what the girls were up to. The girls thought it would be humorous if none of them came into class when the morning bell rang. Part of the regular protocol was that kids would put their backpacks in a row just outside the classroom door and go out to recess before school started. The girls decided, as part of their joke, they wanted me to think that they were all absent that day. They got together before school and stored their backpacks around the side of the school where I wouldn't see them. The next part of their plan involved staying out of sight. When the bell rang to start the school day, the girls all went into the bathroom to hide out.

The boys, for their part, didn't want the girls to pull a fast one on me and kept coming into our room before school to announce what the girls were up to. In addition, they began taking the girls' backpacks and hiding them to play a joke on the girls too. I went into my act right then and told the boys that I didn't care what the girls were up to and that I wasn't about to go try and chase them down. When the bell rang, all of the boys entered the room, but the girls remained hidden. Instead of acting all upset like I guess the boys expected me to be, I began taking the roll as I normally did each day. I called out each student's name and they told me if they wanted hot lunch, cold lunch, or salad bar. Of course, when I called a girl's name, there was dead silence. The boys were confused by what I was doing, since I obviously knew that the girls were not in the room.

I finished roll, and I began with whatever we were doing that day. I really hadn't thought this whole thing out myself, but if it continued much longer, I would have sent someone to tell the girls that they needed to come back to class. About that moment, the girls decided it was time to end their joke, and they all walked in with smirks on their faces carrying their backpacks (apparently, they had figured out where the boys had stashed them). They were really feeling proud of themselves as they strode into class.

At that moment, I moved into my best angry teacher voice impression and told the girls that they were all in trouble. I said the principal was not happy and that she wanted to see them all in the office immediately! Suddenly the smiles evaporated and looks of fear came over some of their faces as this was not something they had thought was going to happen. Just for a brief moment, I felt a touch of guilt because there were a couple of girls who probably had never been in trouble a day in their lives with looks of significant distress on their faces. It was a "what have I done?" moment for them. As they all started to leave the classroom together I said in my most mischievous voice, "April Fools, girls!" They didn't really know how to react after that, but that was one time I got them back really good.

My Biggest Frustrations

It is always better to look at the glass half full than half empty. There were so many great parts about being a teacher, but I would be remiss if I also didn't point out the challenging and difficult things that bring frustration to those of us who always tried to project positivity.

One thing you may come across, on occasion, is the annoying voice of the teacher who is never happy about anything. After what seemed like endless days in a row of constant complaining, I wanted to shout, "Did you ever think that this might not be the right profession for you???"

Thank goodness the vast majority of teachers don't fall into this category because negativity breeds more negativity. If you have two likeminded individuals on your staff who focus on the negative, my advice is to stay out of the staff room as much as possible. When you have more than one person pontificating about what is wrong with education, it's as if they are taking turns pouring gasoline on a fire. I would equate this with two individuals in a marriage who spend the majority of their time fighting or complaining about one another rather than trying to do something constructive to improve the situation.

We all get frustrated and annoyed by what is happening in our school and within the field of education, in general, from time to time. I can almost promise you that there are going to be times when you feel the same way as the teacher who carries on day after day. A poor attitude is not going to solve the problem, but we all need moments and times when we can express our frustrations.

My advice would be to try to find someone else a little further removed from your school to whom you can express your feelings. That might be with a spouse or significant other, best friend, therapist, an online chat group, or even writing in a journal. Utilizing any of these would be healthier than pouring fuel on the fire by engaging in these negative conversations with others at your school who love it when they can wallow in their misery with someone else.

I used to belong to an online chat group of fellow educators. Discussing your frustrations with a group like this is a better approach than continually complaining to your colleagues. Sometimes people further removed can look at a situation more objectively and rationally than a person who is right in the middle of it. Another plus about talking to those entirely independent of your school is that they may offer you advice or share how they dealt with a similar situation. You can consider their ideas to determine if they might work for you.

I happen to share the same profession as my spouse, but we worked in different school districts. Over the years, I taught with a couple of husband and wife duos who worked at the same school. I wondered what their conversations were like at the end of the day. Did they ever decide that after the school day they would not talk about school subjects during their private time?

Even though I enjoyed most school days, there were times I came home in a sour mood. Occasionally, the same feelings occurred for my wife. At times you feel like talking about it, and other times you don't want to relive your rough days. There were those rare days when we both came home and felt like we wanted to pack up and move to some remote tropical island. We never set ground rules about any of this, but there was an understanding between us that we could always talk about our school problems to one another if we felt like it. There were times when I did and other times when I wanted to escape from school for the night and focus on something else. I think my wife felt the same way I did.

A lot of the time I felt better after telling her about my day. We would often end up laughing about the humor or ridiculousness of a situation after we had a chance to vent. One of the best qualities that I inherited from my mom was a sense of humor. I believe in the principle that "laughter is the best medicine," and there were countless times I felt better after sharing a laugh about the absurdities of the school day.

I once had a parent who walked into my class with the materials for a chemistry project. Not only was I in the middle of a lesson when she showed up unannounced (this means she didn't stop in at the office as required but instead went directly to my classroom), but she wanted me to stop everything at that moment because she "thought the class would be interested in watching a chemical reaction." In what planet would anyone think this was an appropriate thing to do? As I joked about this later with a colleague, I said, "She nearly induced a chemical reaction from me." Laughing about such ridiculous moments that went on at school was exactly the right prescription for those times.

Teaching can be a challenging job, even when everything is going well in your personal life. A few years before my retirement, my mom had to move into an assisted living center about thirty minutes away from us. Even though she had great care workers, it was tough to manage her frequent trips in and out of the hospital, and she needed a lot of help getting to and from her many doctor appointments. I had the sweetest mom, and I would do anything for her. It was challenging to meet all of her needs when I had a full-time job, but I did the best I could under the circumstances.

My mother-in-law was going through many of the same issues, but the main difference was that she lived a much further distance away and was still in her home, albeit with 24-hour care. I am a happily married man with an incredibly supportive wife. I know how hard it was at times to manage our busy lives, and we only have one child. I can't even imagine how full-time, working, single parents with three or four kids cope with all of life's challenges.

The ever-changing curriculum can be a frustration that all teachers have to be able to handle. It is a good and healthy thing to have a certain amount of change. I always wondered how anyone could teach the same grade and do the same things year after year, but some people prefer it that way. I supported changes that were made based on sound educational research.

Unfortunately, the reality is that cutting costs, rather than improvements to the program, drives many decisions made in education. Sometimes a curriculum that most of us loved and seemed to be working well was discontinued out of the blue. That often occurred because it was no longer a state adopted program. If the government won't provide any funding because the materials are no longer state approved, then an excellent program that is working well gets discarded purely for economic reasons. On other occasions, a new administrator, with the support of the school board, may decide that he/she wants to use a different curriculum. The shift to a new program sometimes happened because the administrator had used it in his/her previous school and believed this was the right course of action. I understand that an administrator sometimes has to make decisions that aren't always going to be popular, but I felt that the staff was more likely to get on board with a change if they were involved in the process.

State testing is another area of frustration for many teachers, including me. I understand why state assessments exist, and I do feel like there is a place for them. I believe that we place too much emphasis on these tests. Often, the assessments did not match what the kids were learning. I know this may sound like a bitter teacher whose students underachieved on these assessments, but our school traditionally did quite well on these standardized tests. Even when our students did very well on the testing, I felt that they left a lot to be desired and were not a very good indicator of the school's success or failure.

In recent years, the format of the state test has changed significantly. I administered the old test to 2nd-6th graders for nearly thirty years. The kids each had to complete a series of about twelve subtests. There were questions in reading, math, language, spelling, listening, social studies, and science that the students completed in big test booklets at their desks. The items on the test were all multiple-choice style questions, and the students were not overwhelmed by the sheer length of the tests. All of the individual subtests were timed and took forty-five minutes or less to complete. My students had mixed feelings about taking state tests during this era. There were always some kids in the class who enjoyed them, and the kids who didn't care for them still managed to complete the tests without a bunch of frustration and tears. Of course, there was the occasional question about something you hadn't studied yet at that point in the year, but I would assume that every school had this situation. As long as everyone was playing by the same set of rules, it seemed fair enough to me.

My only real complaint at the time was that I felt a lot of 2nd graders lacked the maturity to stay focused for long periods of time. I remember having kids who weren't even 1/3 of the way done with a test who were asking questions like, "How much longer do we have to do this?" If the goal of these tests were to measure how well the kids were learning, I would say the results are more of a reflection of the overall maturity of the kids who are taking the test. I seldom had this problem with many of my older students. As of the past few years, 2nd grade is now exempt from state testing. (It appears that the California Department of Education reached the same conclusion that I did).

The format of the state test changed quite a bit in the last two years of my career. The assessments were now online. In an attempt to get students to think more critically, there was a reduction of multiple choice questions. Kids were asked to type about how they came up with a solution, instead of just answering multiple choice questions. There were allowances made for slower workers, and time limits became a thing of the past.

Some of these changes are well-intended, and their rationale is clear. On the other hand, this kind of new testing had its own set of drawbacks. One of the most noticeable changes was that the students needed to be very computer literate. That, of course, is a necessity in the world today, but they were asked to do things on the computer with which they may have had little or no experience. Kids had to be able to work with split screens, move things around in sequence, highlight or underline specific words or phrases, draw lines across geometric figures, and use other specialized computer skills. The only practice my students received with some of these proficiencies came from the accompanying online practice tests, and many of these skills were new to several of my 3rd graders.

As an administrator of the test, you could not help the kids at all with any issues they encountered. While testing was in progress, sometimes they encountered technical problems and were kicked off in the middle of the tests. (I don't have enough expertise or knowledge to know why this was even happening.) I remember a couple of my students who lost the work they had already done and had to start over on a particular test. That would be frustrating enough for an adult. Try to explain to third graders that they need to start over after they've already been working on an assessment for close to an hour. In my last year of teaching, my third graders were asked to read multiple passages and points of view and state their opinion on a question with support from the different readings. I thought the test, in general, was extremely difficult and not very age-appropriate. As I am writing this, our local paper recently came out with an article stating that only 38% of the students in our county scored proficiently on the test. Someone who was not familiar with the difficulty of the tests might assume that this means our local schools are doing a poor job.

The newer types of assessments have been modified to give students unlimited time to complete the tests. This sounds good in theory, but giving kids additional time to do something they may not know how to do in the first place isn't going to help them be more successful. I would equate it to a layperson being given extra time to rebuild a car engine. Giving me extra time to do a job like that isn't going to help me be successful since I lack the expertise in knowing how to complete the task in the first place. If anything, I think it would cause a person even greater frustration.

Another problem with state testing is the considerable emphasis that some schools will, quite naturally, place on these tests. When people think that one school is better than another because it has higher test scores, they are not taking into account the many other factors that one overall measure can't reveal. Some schools are going to put a much greater emphasis on these tests. This means that some will start focusing on testing weeks ahead of time, while others don't practice at all and continue to teach the regular curriculum right up to the start of testing. If one school is practicing for the test for several weeks, then it follows that their test scores are more likely to be higher than a school that doesn't put such an emphasis into this. The socioeconomic level of the families who live in that particular school district can also affect scores. It is not that surprising that schools with higher socioeconomic profiles generally do better just because these kids often have more resources and may come from homes where education is stressed more. Kids who come from more impoverished families tend to be more transient, and it is difficult for children who go in and out of multiple schools.

I also think that it is vital that we always keep the best interests of our students at the forefront of any educational decisions that we make. There were times I felt physically sick when I saw the emotional burden that we were placing on students regarding testing. There is such a pressure to do well on the assessments that some of this angst is inadvertently passed on to kids by stressed-out teachers. One can tell kids to relax and do their best when taking state assessments, but how does this match the feeling that was passed on to teachers that your test scores determine the success or failure of a school year? Putting a tremendous emphasis on improving test scores, when kids need their basic necessities in life met seems crazy and disproportionate. You teach kids that don't even know where they are going to be sleeping that night or whether they're going to go hungry, and yet we want them to care about some test that has no bearing on their lives?

To summarize my thoughts on testing, I do think there is a place for them. Testing can reveal areas in which your school is doing well or underperforming. At the same time, it is inevitable that many people will conclude that one school is better than another because it has higher test scores. I have heard some of my administrators over the years claim that our emphasis was on "educating and nurturing the whole child," but there were times I felt the approach to testing didn't match the rhetoric. Our primary responsibility as educators is to always look out for the welfare of our students, and there is something substantially wrong when we give assessments that bring children to tears and make them feel bad about themselves. I would hope that the state government will continue to look for ways to improve the quality of the testing program. We must have fairer and improved tests that are a better reflection of what kids are learning. We shouldn't be so hasty to make broad generalizations from the data, and we need to look at other ways to measure a school's success besides state tests.

As I said, change is good; however, too many changes at once leads to a staff of stressed-out teachers. You might be surprised at all of the changes that will take place at the local, state, and national level. Near the end of my career, there was a push toward Common Core, which was an educational initiative in the United States that detailed what K-12 students should know in language arts and mathematics at the end of each grade. In California, we used to refer to this as the grade level standards.

My wish is that schools would choose something and stick with it. I know our school invested a lot of time and energy into Common Core when it became apparent that this would be our teaching guideline. We spent many staff meetings and invested many hours looking over the Common Core guides and tried to incorporate literature across the curriculum to fit this model. I am not saying Common Core was/is the end-all, be-all program. There were things that I liked and didn't like about it. We were encouraged to go into more detail and depth with the kids regarding the material that they were learning. That was a good thing. On so many occasions in the past, I felt like we moved on prematurely before the majority of the kids had mastered a skill because there was just so much left for us to cover. When we began using Common Core, I think we may have covered less ground, but I felt the kids were learning the concepts in greater detail.

My last year of teaching was the beginning of the election cycle. We began to hear from politicians that we needed to do away with Common Core. My frustration came not from a belief that this was the gospel of teaching as much as it was, "now what are we going to do?" I was frustrated with a lot of aspects regarding the No Child Left Behind approach, but my initial thought when I was about to retire was feeling happy that I didn't have to be part of another revolutionary change in education. I wish we'd find something that works and stick with it for more than one or two election cycles.

In the last two years that I taught, we adopted a new language arts program called <u>Success for All</u>. It was the second time in my tenure that we used this program. Every student in the school had language arts for ninety minutes. It was the same time each day of school. One part of this program that appealed to me was the placement of children into their reading groups. Placing kids into groups on ability level rather than chronological age makes more sense. Just about any teacher would tell you that it is much easier to teach a group of kids when they perform at similar ability levels. One part of Success for All (SFA) that didn't match Common Core for me was that SFA was very scripted. There were a regular cycle and schedule for us to follow that did not allow for much latitude from their program. Where Common Core encouraged us to go into subjects more deeply, SFA's focus was on getting through the scheduled lesson each day.

As with just about any new program, some of my colleagues liked SFA while others did not. There were things about SFA that I thought were good, but there were also elements that I thought could be improved upon or eliminated. One of the most frustrating parts for me was continually having to enter data into my computer. As an experienced teacher, I knew what was working and what wasn't. I didn't need to submit hours of data to determine what I already knew. A good teacher makes adjustments from year to year and even day to day based on what is working and not working. I don't think that SFA and Common Core aligned well with one another.

In your school, always try to improve your teaching and the methods by which you are teaching. There is a saturation point when you try to take on too many new things at once. You may feel like you're still trying to perfect the changes that you implemented the previous year. Not only are changes happening every year, but the resources to implement these are decreasing. When I first began working in schools, before I had my teaching credential, every classroom in my former district had teacher's aides. There were school nurses, librarians, music teachers, art teachers, physical education instructors, school psychologists/counselors who often worked exclusively at one school rather than being shared by many schools as often is the case today. These services have slowly evaporated to the point they may now be part-time or have disappeared altogether. Over time more and more of these things were taken over by the classroom teacher. Teachers were being asked to do more with fewer resources. While I always felt that I made a respectable wage as a teacher, there were a lot of years that we didn't get any raise. In fact, teacher salaries often wouldn't keep up with the cost of living while we were being asked to do more.

The general public would be amazed to learn how much money most teachers spend on materials for their classrooms. In California, we received reimbursement for some of these dollars from our state lottery, but that was just a small fraction of what most teachers spend. Generally, the school purchased the basic supplies that all students needed such as paper, pencils, scissors, glue, etc. These purchases happen before school starts and often the budget was so fixed that when the materials ran out, we went without or purchased them ourselves. In a typical school year, I went to an office supply store at least once a week to buy something for my classroom. By the end of the year, my receipts often totaled over $1,000. That meant I was spending over $100 per month (10 months of school) on my students and classroom. Some years I spent as much as $2,000 for my class. I also bought some incentives throughout the year for my students.

Teachers use their funds all the time! That is just the reality of the situation. What other industry asks the employees to do anything remotely similar to this?

Many parents have no idea about all of the extra contributions that most teachers make so that their school can be a better place for kids to learn. While the parents who are more involved in the school have a better idea of what is happening, many things go unnoticed. All of the volunteer hours and extraordinary commitment to students are a staple of most teachers. I spent part of Saturday at school nearly every weekend during the school year. I didn't do it because I was paid to be there. I did it because I felt I needed to invest this time to do my job adequately. I was not the only one on my staff who did this. In fact, it got to be kind of a joke among the regulars who used to run into each other down at school on the weekends. I used to chuckle to myself when a parent would happen to be at the school on the weekend with their child and innocently ask, "What are you doing here? It's Saturday."

I just smiled, but inside there was a part of me that wanted to answer, "I've been here every Saturday during the school year for the last twenty-five years!" Just because teachers aren't at school on the weekend doesn't mean they aren't working on schoolwork from home. I had plenty of colleagues who just took home a lot of work with them.

Teachers are blessed to have several weeks in the summer to recharge their batteries, but once again a lot of the public has no idea of all of the extra hours that most teachers devote to school, even during the summer. Many teachers take classes or workshops, and it was not unusual to go into work on some random day in the summer and run into a few other people who happened to come into school to work on something. Summertime for me was my catch-up time around school. I would go through my file cabinets, build something for my classroom, look through new teaching materials to become more familiar with a program, and numerous other things.

I was always looking for ways to help my school outside my

regular contracted hours. I helped install two new playground modules at Pine Hill and one at our sister school (South Bay). Three times I built the ball walls at my school (either alone or with the assistance of colleagues, parents, and even students). I served as the Student Council teacher/liaison at my school (unpaid) for many years. The kids and I frequently took on some projects to improve the campus, including painting the lines for all of the games on the school playground. We raised money by holding car washes, ice cream socials, popcorn sales, and whatever other ideas we could come up with to help fund these improvements. We also worked on some community service project. One of the things I did with the kids was work at a local animal shelter. Many times, parents are thrilled to help out with these kinds of things too. They want to help in their child's school, but they don't know how. Why not take advantage of this resource when you can?

I often took on projects with my students to contribute to those who were in need. We held popcorn sales to raise money for earthquake or hurricane victims. We didn't raise much money, but the kids were learning to do what they could to help the community and the world.

One of our teachers used to teach an elementary choir after school for kids from K-3rd grades. I liked to sing and help out with this group too. Around the holidays, the kids would perform at care homes in the evenings or on Saturdays.

I wrote a grant to have the playground resurfaced and to have four new basketball standards purchased. Some of my fellow teachers and I came on the weekend and drilled the holes for the basketball poles with an auger, cemented the large poles into the ground, and came back the following day to install the backboards, rims, and nets. I did this voluntarily because I saw a situation that I had the expertise with which to help, and I knew that our playground could use some improvements. Once again, this was a perfect opportunity to involve some parent volunteers, and I would have recruited some if I didn't get the help of some of my fellow staff members.

A pair of my fellow teachers/friends at Pine Hill took it upon themselves to put in a school garden. They worked on this for something like fifteen weekends after writing a grant to help pay for the development. That included rototilling the land, putting in raised beds for each of the classrooms, laying down fabric over the ground, putting wood chips over the fabric, installing a drip system, putting in a compost bin, and helping to find a curriculum that the staff could use. It was an enormous task, and some parents and staff members helped, but without the leadership, energy, and passion of these two fantastic teachers, the garden project would not have happened. Sometimes we're reluctant to ask for help or bother parents, but some of those parents who couldn't help during the week because of their job might be able to meet on a Saturday to contribute some labor or expertise.

Another time commitment that usually goes unnoticed by the parental community is all of the committees in which most teachers serve. They are often formed to assess how the school is doing in many different areas. For example, we implemented a new behavior plan in our school and frequently met to see what was working and what needed modification. When a new reading program began, we held regular meetings to assess its effectiveness. We had a Safety Committee who reviewed disaster and earthquake preparedness. Committees or individual teachers were in charge of the Science Fair or History Day for our upper-grade students. There are many more committees as well because there is always something to evaluate and improve. These committee meetings took place during our regularly scheduled workday. In effect, this meant our other regular duties just got pushed back outside of our contracted hours. Consequently, I was grading papers, making parent phone calls that needed to be made, or working on future lessons for the following day on my own time because these were all things that were necessary.

Our school had a Parent Teacher Organization (PTO). This group met monthly in the evenings and was usually planning some fundraiser, family/school event, or school improvement project to be held in the evening or on the weekend. This group was just another of the many happenings that took place in a regular school year. In my eyes, this was a really critical group to make the school an even better place, but the reality is that at some point everyone hits the wall and something has to give. Unfortunately, not very many teachers were active in this group. It didn't mean they were uncaring--just that they were continually giving up their own free and family time when they were already putting an enormous amount of energy into their jobs. Another sad reality is that not many parents were active in our parent/teacher group. As someone who regularly tried to participate in this group, I witnessed the same cycle happen many times among the parents. We usually had a modest group of parents and teachers who were involved, and the parents who often had to take a leadership role burned out. Then the following year we'd get a new small group of involved parents, who often had full-time jobs themselves, that took on more than they could manage, and the cycle just repeated itself.

Even the most dedicated teachers and parents reach a saturation point where it just gets to be too much. There would be weekends in which I just felt I didn't have enough time to recharge my batteries. After teaching all week and giving my all, I remember volunteering by showing up Friday night to crack eggs with a small group of parents and getting things ready for the following morning's pancake breakfast. Then I'd volunteer three hours to work at the pancake breakfast at the crack of dawn Saturday morning. I'd usually go in and work in my classroom for three to four hours on Saturday mornings, but because of the breakfast, I postponed this until Sunday. Somewhere in my "free time" I would be correcting papers, taking my son to football practice, and mowing the lawn at home. Monday would roll around, and one of my colleagues would ask how my weekend went. I tried to remain positive and present a good attitude, but inside I was thinking, "I'm so tired from everything that I don't feel like I've even had a weekend."

I never focused on how many extra hours I was working at school because in my eyes I was doing what was necessary to do the job well.

I felt that I was earning a decent living, doing something important, and making my community a better place. In California, we are entering a crisis phase because there is a tremendous teacher shortage. Fewer people are entering the profession because a lot of young people are finding more financially rewarding paths. While the majority of parents are supportive, there are others who take no responsibility toward their child's education. They feel that is entirely up to the school and the teacher to deal with their child's education and will even speak openly and express these feelings aloud. "This isn't my job. It is your job to get my child to learn."

It is no mystery why so many young teachers leave the profession early on when they feel unsupported or underappreciated. When parents don't offer any support, children learn there are fewer and fewer consequences for their actions. When public education becomes the scapegoat and target of so much misinformation written about by many different sources, it affects the way you feel about your job. You know that you are giving 100% maximum effort, and yet it feels like your efforts aren't being recognized, or even worse, are being criticized. It can be downright discouraging!

One of the hardest things about being a teacher was having to come to school and plan for a substitute when I was sick. In most jobs, you can make a phone call and let your employer know that you won't be coming in that day. As a teacher, I felt a tremendous responsibility to get myself to school even when I was running a fever or throwing up. I felt an obligation to write a lesson plan and get the necessary teaching materials ready for the substitute. That preparation would often take up to two hours for just one day.

If you know you are going to miss school to attend a workshop, then you have the luxury of getting some things ready days ahead of time. What many people probably don't realize though is that a teacher's plans are adjusted day by day. Sometimes you discover that your class failed to understand an important concept, and you must spend time reteaching it to them. Lots of times an average school day can be disrupted by an array of things, many of which you have no control over. There was a head lice outbreak, and time was needed to be made to check students' heads. Occasionally, the administrator would neglect to tell us that a speaker was coming to do an assembly later that day. One of my pet peeves was when we had Picture Day at our school (at least twice a year), and the teacher would have no idea when it was going to be his class's turn. We were just expected to drop whatever we were doing at that moment to get our pictures taken. That was extremely frustrating, and the kids would tend to get pretty wound up on days like this. I couldn't help but see the mixed message of having a philosophy of not wanting anything to interfere with the students' learning, and yet we allowed Picture Day to disrupt whatever was happening. The point is that the lesson plan for one day will get altered for the following day based on something that happened. A teacher can write a plan for the week ahead of time, but without fail, the plan changes many times throughout the week.

If I got sick during the night, then I knew that I would have to get in to work as early as possible to get things ready for the substitute. On one occasion I can remember lying in bed and realizing that I was not going to be able to teach that day. I was worried about all of the things that I needed to do; consequently, I got up at 3:00 a.m. and drove to school. Because I wasn't thinking clearly, I went directly to my classroom and neglected to turn off the alarm for the school. Seconds later the alarm was blaring, and I was rushing down to the staff room to punch in the code to turn it off. Part of the protocol was that a teacher had to call the alarm company if you ever set off the alarm. You did this immediately, otherwise; the alarm company would dispatch the police to the school.

I often wondered what the alarm company worker must have thought when I called her at 3:30 a.m. to tell her that I was down at school and had set off the alarm by accident. I'm sure she was trained to handle each situation without questioning why someone set off the alarm, but she had to be thinking, "What are you doing at school at this hour?" I have worked for administrators who wanted us to have a week's worth of emergency sub plans. While this could be time-consuming, I can understand why an administrator would ask a teacher to do this. Sub plans vary quite a bit from teacher to teacher, and I heard horror stories in which a teacher left virtually no plans at all. (sometimes because of real emergencies) That wouldn't be fair to a substitute, or the class for that matter. Having emergency lesson plans to draw on would at least enable a sub to get through a day.

One of the other things that have changed over the years has been the addition of after-school programs. When I first started teaching, after-school programs within the school did not exist. I am not speaking out against these programs because they benefit so many kids and their families. In today's society, with so many parents both working, after-school programs are almost a necessity.

The after-school program at our school was fabulous! Kids could receive homework help, physical exercise, healthy foods, and enrichment classes when they finished their schoolwork, and all of these things were great. What wasn't fabulous was that there were so many children who attended these programs (more than 50% of the kids in the school) that space to house them became difficult. Because of the overall lack of space in a school, it became necessary to use the regular school classrooms to accommodate all of the children. There were after-school workers hired for these positions, but often they lacked training, and sometimes their classroom management abilities were insufficient. I wanted to work in my classroom, but, depending on who the supervisor was, I often had to leave and try to find another quiet spot on the campus. I also liked to work with children after school in tutoring sessions, but there were times when it was nearly impossible to find a quiet area anywhere. When I did remain in my room and tried to work through the excessive noise, I sometimes had a hard time not intervening when the person in charge lacked any classroom management skills. For a couple of years, during parent-teacher conferences, I had to move to another room to conduct the meetings because the after-school program needed my classroom. That meant carrying everything I needed for the five conferences that I would be hosting that day. The portable room I was given to use was hard for the parents to find, and it was an extra pain having to transport everything I wanted to share at the conferences.

A frustration for the administration and teachers is that we are reaching a crisis point in the number of qualified teachers in the area. When I first was hired, there was somewhere in the neighborhood of one hundred applicants for my job. We live in a beautiful location near a college town, and many people stayed in the area after graduating. What has evolved over the last several years in California, and in other regions of the United States as well, is that we are facing a teacher shortage. The number of teachers coming out of the teacher preparation program at our local university this past year was far below the number of teachers who retired in our county. What has happened in the last few years is there aren't enough qualified people, and this worries me about the future of education. I think one of three scenarios is going to take place in the coming years in an attempt to reverse this shortage of teachers: (1) Increased efforts will go toward recruiting more young people into the field of education. (2) Lowered standards for obtaining a teaching credential will lead to less qualified teachers. (3) Teacher salaries will be raised significantly so that more young people consider teaching as an attractive profession.

I think the last scenario is the least likely of these three choices. We haven't had a healthy supply of substitute teachers to meet the demand the last few years. It is extremely difficult from a teacher's perspective to miss one day or more of school. The sad reality is that teachers who really should stay home when they are ill come to school because preparing a sub-plan is almost more trouble than just being there when you aren't 100%. Substitutes are woefully underpaid for such a hard job. Walking into a classroom and looking at a lesson plan for a few minutes before school hardly prepares you for what lies ahead that day. Substitutes may have little to no background with a particular group of kids and be unaware of some very serious behavior problems. The number of teachers on the available sub list was so short that our principal often ended up teaching a class. Many principals have teaching experience, and at least they are familiar with the kids in the school. On the other hand, if they are teaching, then how do they adequately address the different facets of their administrative job? That was not unique to my district. My wife's school had the same problem. She was in charge of contacting substitutes when one of her teachers called in sick. If she couldn't get enough help, then she had to take the place of the teacher.

If we want more young people to consider going into teaching, then one of the things that are going to have to change is the attitudes toward teachers and public education in our society. There are examples of failing teachers and schools in America, but the vast majority of schools are doing a great job with inadequate resources. One of the things that I find especially distressing these days is the fact that there seems to be an increased tolerance from schools toward insubordinate behavior. Students are learning that there are fewer and fewer consequences for their actions. The families of expelled children have sued school districts when the school is attempting to create a safe environment for the rest of the students.

The law is that everyone has a right to an education, and I think this is a good thing. On the other hand, at what point is the right of students who want to learn being infringed upon by children who disrupt their learning? I know I've heard more and more from other teachers who have told horror stories about their district discouraging them from suspending children. When a student talks back or even threatens another student or adult in the school without consequences, what kind of message does this send to the students?

One cultural difference I experienced as a teacher was the positive attitudes that I almost always felt from many of my non-native English students and their parents. By valuing education within a culture, the accompanying attitudes toward teachers will also follow suit. Teachers want to feel they are appreciated and valued. Part of this is making the profession more attractive from a financial point of view, but it also has to do with developing an attitude throughout society that teachers deserve respect for the difficult job they are doing.

Final Thoughts

I have absolutely no regrets about choosing to become a teacher. I made friends and memories that will last a lifetime. The majority of people that enter the business of education are terrific people. I felt like I was given the rarest of gifts to make a positive contribution to society each day I walked into my classroom.

One of my most significant concerns for the future of education in California and throughout the country has to do with the dwindling number of people who are entering this field. The logical question is, why is this happening? While I still believe the majority of people don't get into this profession for the money, I think the sad reality is that many young people have found that there are easier ways to make a buck. The job of being a teacher continues to get more challenging all the time.

I know that when I began teaching, I learned that the average career for a teacher lasted only seven years. It is sad that so many young people who enter the profession appear to be getting out because they are discouraged by all of the obstacles they face. The demands are great, and the stress is real. While I loved my career, I ultimately decided to retire because I felt that I needed to focus on taking better care of myself. I put 100% into my students and my school, but the constant grind took a toll on me physically. I got pneumonia one year and missed several weeks of school. While I lay in bed on Christmas for the 3rd year in a row, I decided it was time to listen to my body and call it a career at the end of that school year.

One of my core beliefs is that people of all ages need role models. My two most influential role models in education, Cynthia Van Vleck and Nancy Wheeler, influenced me so much in my student teaching year and throughout my entire career. They were two of the most outstanding teachers and people I have ever met, and I always felt that if I could be half the teacher they were, I would be a very successful educator. The people that we admire and look up to inspire and make us want to be better at our craft.

Many of your students come to school and have family members or friends that are a positive influence on them, but what about all of your other students who don't have anyone in their life to guide or inspire them? That is where teachers can make their most significant impact.

Every teacher, especially young teachers, should be supported by one another. Education works best when you are all working as a team. Experienced teachers should look out for younger teachers that may need more support. Newer teachers should look for role models and support from their colleagues rather than trying to prove their worth. Administrators can help facilitate this by encouraging experienced staff members to take their more inexperienced counterparts under their wings. A capable administrator looks out for all of the people in the school, including the children and the staff. Many teachers, including myself, begin their careers with idealistic goals. At some point, the day to day realities of education may lessen this idealism some, but hopefully, you will always carry that belief that you have the power and ability to change lives.

When I think back to my education, there were teachers I had who made a tremendous impact on me and some that made no impression at all. In fact, some elementary school years are vacant years in my memory bank. I don't know whether that says something more about those teachers or more about a guy who has a failing memory. The teachers that I do remember are the ones who made me want to be a better student and person. They were the ones who got me to think about other things besides myself. They were the ones who taught me that it was my responsibility to care about the world and to try to leave some lasting legacy for future generations.

I have witnessed other teachers have a tremendous influence on their students, and one, in particular, had an enormous impact on our son. When he was entering 7th grade, he decided that he wanted to play football. Many of his friends were already playing, and I knew this was something that was important to him. When he first began, it was a bit of a struggle for him physically. He was a bigger kid, and he also had the disadvantage of having never played football before. For anyone who has ever watched one of your children play sports, you know how hard this can be from the parental point of view. Of course, you want your child to do well and to have fun. When he/she is struggling, it can be a tough thing for a parent. You want to support your child and to make sure, above all, that it is a positive experience. As parents, my wife and I had always encouraged our son to finish anything he started. There were times when we wondered if it was too much for him and questioned if we were even doing the right thing by encouraging him because he would come home bruised, sore, and discouraged after some of those early practices.

When the games began, the youth league had a rule that every player had to be in the game for at least six plays. There were parent volunteers who monitored this, and the first year he played he was always in for his six plays, but nothing more. My wife and I felt relieved when he finished that year, and I assumed that he wouldn't be interested in playing the following year. He played baseball and basketball in youth sports and also participated in youth soccer one year. After the soccer season ended, he never showed much interest in that sport again, and I figured that football would probably be that way for him too.

That is where being inspired by someone made a difference for him. One of his youth football coaches that year started inviting him over to work out after school at his house. It seemed to be a positive relationship, but there was a small part of us that was concerned because we didn't know this coach very well. It seemed odd that a young guy in his early twenties would take an interest in helping our boy when it wasn't even football season. Our son was motivated and wanted to do this with him, so it continued for a good part of the offseason. In 8th grade, he was a lot stronger, and he had a year of experience under his belt. He began playing a lot more (both offense and defense), and I could see his confidence soar.

When high school began, he continued to play football. He often worked out after school or before school. He had to prove himself at each level as he progressed. In high school he met a teacher/coach who made a tremendous impression on him and ultimately became an incredible role model for him. Having attended a few parental nights over the years when football was about to start each year, I understood why my son wanted to play for this coach. Coach Montana said all the kinds of things that any parent would want to hear. He stressed hard work, doing well in school, and being part of a team. He was such a natural, charismatic, very motivational speaker, and I could clearly understand why so many of the kids, including our son, looked up to him. In fact, I used to walk out of those first parent nights telling my wife that I felt like suiting up for football. Of course, I was joking, but he had that effect on people when he spoke.

Throughout high school, our son worked out either before or after school. He also was doing very well in school and taking many AP advanced classes. At the start of his senior year, he was chosen to be one of the team captains. We were extremely proud of him, mainly because he had accomplished a lot in football. His growth occurred as a result of an excellent work ethic. His football coach/mentor helped bring this out in him, and we were grateful because it was clear how good our son was feeling about himself. He had gone from a player who rarely saw the field to be a starter and team captain. He started regularly hanging out at the coach's house during high school along with several other kids, and I know how much our son looked up to his head coach.

When his last high school game ended, he walked off the field that night and told his mom and me that he wasn't done with football and wanted to continue playing it in college. No athletic scholarships were coming his way, but he was a smart young man, and he was able to earn a partial academic scholarship. In fact, I always felt that what he sometimes lacked in athletic talent, he made up for because of his work ethic and intelligence on the field. He went to an academic school and played Division 3 football.

Once again, I watched the cycle as he went from a player who rarely played as a freshman, only to become a starter in his junior and senior years. He worked hard and continued to develop. He became an all-conference selection his junior and senior years and was a team captain his senior year. Each time when he came back on a school break, my wife and I joked about whether he'd go home and see us first before he went over to visit with his old coach. I know how significant this relationship was and continues to be for our son. Coach Montana was the best role model for our son, and we are so grateful for his positive influence. Throughout his college years, the two of them remained in contact. In fact, I don't think I am exaggerating when I say that our son may have decided to get his degree in exercise science and has since become a college football coach because of the impact that this teacher/coach had on him.

I can't emphasize enough how much influence teachers can have on their students. I have seen it time and time again watching many students flourish and go on to do great things because they had a good role model in their lives. A teacher fills so many roles on a daily basis besides filling the primary role as an educator hired to teach a designated curriculum. Sometimes I felt I was a counselor as much as anything when a child came to school and some very traumatic event had just occurred or he/she was in the middle of facing. People have no idea of the challenging and heartbreaking things that a teacher hears about on a weekly basis from the students. Sometimes the kids come to school, and the parents haven't let you know ahead of time about stressful events that the family is going through right then. Indeed, some parents do, but at other times they probably are unsure about what to do or are in the midst of the personal crisis themselves.

I have had kids break down in class–upset for very valid reasons. When a child starts to sob and tells you his dog died, when he's frightened because his grandma is in the hospital, when a child's parent or loved one is arrested, when the child has learned that her parents are going to be divorced, when a student has just found out her aunt has cancer, you have to be there ready to act. There are so many instances when you suddenly are serving as a social worker, a counselor, an advisor, a friend, or an advocate for a child in an abusive situation. You suddenly are forced to offer the child support because the school may not have the services that a student needs at that moment. The counselor is out sick, at the other school today, on jury duty, at a workshop, etc. We won't have a school nurse coming in until next month. The principal got called away on an emergency. In many cases, it wasn't anyone's fault, but I felt as if I was the lifeline for my students because of the limited resources and people that my school may have had at that particular moment.

New teachers need to realize that there is a big learning curve once you start the job. There is no substitute for practical experience, and you will learn an awful lot about education and kids during your first couple of years in teaching. Education classes can be helpful, but the real learning takes place when you are on the front lines of the classroom each day.

My advice to young people entering the field of education is also to remember to try and make some time for yourself. Even though there are always things to work on at school (seven days a week if you want to), what good are you doing to yourself or your students in the long run if you work so hard that you eventually wear down and get sick? I was always good at giving this advice, but I did not live it that well over the course of my career. Even though I loved teaching right up to my last year, this ultimately is what caused me to retire.

I know that getting out and exercising always made me feel better, physically and mentally, but as the years went by and I put on some weight, this became harder and harder for me to do. What frequently happened is I would overwork and not take care of myself as much as I should have. I eventually got worn down physically and could be out with an illness for extended periods. When I took an honest and hard look at myself, I finally decided after thirty-one years of teaching that I needed to retire and take better care of myself. While I miss the kids and my colleagues, I don't miss the daily grind. I have more energy since I retired, and I am doing a much better job now of taking care of me. My health has dramatically improved, I've lost a lot of weight, and I am rarely sick now. I still go back to school on occasion and volunteer and help out as needed, but I'm also involved in other ways to help my community.

All teachers need to find a way to balance their professional and personal lives. If you are starting out, realize that just learning to manage your class is plenty to look after at the beginning of your career. As you gain experience, you will be able to take on more responsibilities, but initially, cut yourself a break. The last thing you need, especially in your first couple of years, is to try and be Superman or Supergirl. You will be plenty busy just managing your classroom.

One thing that allowed me to retire at age fifty-seven was the fact that my wife and I both started putting money into a tax-sheltered retirement account and kept doing so from the 2nd year of our careers until the point that we both retired. We are living comfortably now and just enjoying life. I know it seems impossible to save money when you are a young teacher just starting out, paying bills, and repaying student loans, but I am so thankful that I followed this advice from some of my more experienced colleagues. Putting some money away into a tax shelter each month just became a way of life for us. If the funds automatically were withdrawn and placed into our respective accounts, we didn't even miss it. Over the years our nest egg grew, and we were able to put our son through college, buy a beautiful home, travel, live comfortably, and yet retire at a young age. I have a lot of things that I still want to do in my life, and I am grateful to be still relatively young.

It is human nature to act like you've got everything under control all of the time, but it's healthier, in the long run, to admit to your boss, colleagues, and even your students' parents when you're having a difficult time in your personal life. They can all offer you support and lend an ear when you need someone to listen. Some people might consider it a sign of weakness to admit when you are having a personal problem, but it is important to recognize when you need a day off. Most teacher contracts have a certain amount of personal necessity days built into them, and sometimes you have to realize that you're helping your students and yourself when you occasionally take a day off.

Since retiring, my wife and I have entered a new phase and are thoroughly enjoying our lives. I have always had a dream of writing children's literature, and I intend to pursue that goal now. In fact, I had no idea that this would all come flowing out of me because the idea of writing a book about my life as a teacher was never something I even considered. Writing this book has been my way of letting go of that period of my life. I have been inspired by two of my former colleagues, Joan and Brenda, who are two of the most giving people I know, and I am following in their footsteps by volunteering for an organization which reads printed material for the visually impaired.

If there were one thing that I wish my readers would glean from my thoughts on education, it would be to understand what a profound influence that a teacher can have on his/her students. You are inspiring and empowering the next generation. Some of your students will go on to do great things because of you! How many people in the world can say that? I've had former students who have chosen this same path, and I couldn't be prouder of them because I know what we do is truly important. Like a mama bear protects her cubs, I get very defensive when I hear public schools and teachers getting a bad rap. So much of the criticism that I hear and read often comes from people who aren't even aware of the tremendous sacrifices that most teachers make for their students and their schools. I know, and I wish I could give all of you a standing ovation. You are all my heroes and heroines because it takes a lot of heart to be a good teacher! Teaching is a skilled craft, and I wish I had a dollar for every time I had a parent who volunteered in my room say to me, "I don't know how you do this." Well, I did it, and I loved it! Next, to my family, there is nothing in my life that makes me prouder!

Appendix

I Have a Problem

Your Name _____

Today's Date _____

Describe the problem. (Be specific)

_____

_____

_____

_____

_____

How did you try to solve the problem?

_____

_____

_____

_____

_____

Friendship Club

Your Name _____

Today's Date _____

Who did something nice for you?
_____

Describe how that person was a good friend.
_____
_____
_____
_____
_____
_____
_____
_____
_____
_____

Weekly Report for_____

Homework Completed

Day of the Week	Homework Completed	Homework Not Completed
Monday	_____	_____
Tuesday	_____	_____
Wednesday	_____	_____
Thursday	_____	_____
Friday	_____	_____

Behavior

Day of Week	Excellent	Warning	Teacher Conference	Miss One Recess	Call Parent & Visit Principal
Monday	_____	_____	_____	_____	_____
Tuesday	_____	_____	_____	_____	_____
Wednesday	_____	_____	_____	_____	_____
Thursday	_____	_____	_____	_____	_____
Friday	_____	_____	_____	_____	_____

Recent Grades

Math Chapter 5 Test   _____   Spelling Test _____
Social Studies Project _____

Other Notes

We have been learning about geometrical shapes in math. The kids were responsible for learning all of the shapes on the study guide I gave them. This week the kids will be drawing mathematical shapes to the nearest quarter inch with a ruler. In social studies we have been learning about important inventions from the 19th century. A project that I am going to have the kids working on in class this week is to have them develop an idea for an invention that they would like to see in the future. They will be bringing home an assignment sheet on Wed. that further describes the project. The kids will be conducting interviews of an assigned partner for language arts next week. Their job this week is to come up with a list of 15 questions that they would like to ask their interview partner. These questions should either be typed on the computer or written in the student's best printing/handwriting. This is due Friday. All of these things are in their homework folders.

Parent Signature (Return by Wednesday) _____

CPSIA information can be obtained
at www.ICGtesting.com
Printed in the USA
BVHW041709140720
583606BV00006B/396